That Last Glorious Summer
1939
Shanghai ⟺ Japan

That Last Glorious Summer
1939
Shanghai ⟺ Japan

Rena Krasno

Edited
by
Tess Johnston

Old China Hand Press
Hong Kong

Cover: Rena, her sister Alla, and two friends by the sea in Japan

Edited by Tess Johnston
Old China Hand Research Service
1202/905 Huai Hai Zhong Lu
Shanghai 200031, China

Book Design by Deke Erh

Published by
Old China Hand Press (Hong Kong)
Shanghai Office:
210/2 Taikang Lu
Shanghai 200025, China

ISBN No. 962-7872-17-2

Address inquiries to:
Rena Krasno, 255 S. Rengstorff, #106,
Mountain View, CA 94040, USA.

Published and printed in Hong Kong.

To My Friends:

Genny Topas Bloch, in memory of her father Boris Topas, who sacrificed his life for the Shanghai Jewish Community; Fernande and Paul Monnot, for their memories and material; and Edith Jane Benay, for her unflinching loyalty and dedication.

To My friends:

Chapter 1

In the summer of 1939, my mother sought temporary respite from the disturbances in Shanghai by taking my sister and me on a vacation to Japan. My father was employed by a British trading firm and could not take leave to accompany us. Prior to our departure, the family discussions centered mainly on our finances which, although not grim, were far from brilliant. We agreed that we could afford tourist class steamer tickets and could save on our rent by sharing a seaside cottage with a Japanese family. The offer of a cottage was made to my mother by the Noritake China agent in Shanghai; he was a Japanese gentleman, born in Canada, with whom my mother had had some business dealings and whom she grew to like and trust. His lyrical descriptions of the delicate beauty of the Japanese landscape and the peaceful rural life of villagers had enchanted her. My mother was an enterprising and rather adventurous young woman — she was 35 at the time — and immediately set about acquiring the necessary Stateless Russian Refugee Travel Certificates. We had neither citizenship nor passports from any country.

In 1921, as a young man of 22, my father had left Vladivostok in Russia's Far East. He was on his way to Palestine with a group of passionate but penniless Zionists, who stopped in Shanghai on the first lap of their journey. Unfortunately, my father had an acute attack of appendicitis and had to be hospitalized in Shanghai. His friends proceeded to Palestine and to future fame as founders of the Jerusalem Cultural Center and the Dead Sea Chemical Works while my disappointed father underwent surgery in Shanghai. He was not able to reach Israel, the destination of his dreams, until April 1949.

When I was young, my father seemed to me the handsomest

man in the world. I loved his curly brown hair, his straight nose and his increasingly sad eyes as the Nazi terror grew in Europe. He devoted all his spare time, energy and thought to Jewish problems and took his duties as the Honorary Secretary of the Shanghai Ashkenazi Jewish Community very seriously. When Jewish refugees fleeing the Holocaust started arriving in Shanghai in 1937, he became a dedicated member of the various committees that came to their aid.

My father was a modest man, a talented and surprisingly passionate writer, a rather shy reader (in public) of his excellent poems and a devoted worker for the good of society. He tried — not always successfully — to keep his quick temper under control. Injustice, narrow-mindedness, selfishness, greed, petty bickering and rivalry infuriated him. We both loved literature, and my father always amazed me, not only by reciting long Russian poems by heart, but also by his knowledge of European and American authors whom he had read in Russian translation. One of our closest moments was on a cold, drizzly day when we stood together as the Russian community of Shanghai unveiled a monument to Pushkin in the French Concession.

In 1935, my father published in Shanghai a book of poems in Russian, which remained his mother tongue. The title was *The Wide Open Heart,* and it was dedicated "To My Children." Rather shyly, my father had handed me a copy, which he had bound himself in printed cloth. On the inside of the cover were the words:

"To my daughter Irochka. I hope one day you will understand me."

I had mumbled, "Thank you," holding back a fervid response: "I do! I do!"

My mother was a kind woman with optimism, imagination, and an indomitable zest for life. She had come to Shanghai from Siberia at the age of six with her parents and siblings.

Shortly afterward, her father died in a cholera epidemic. Her mother had supported her seven children by preparing and serving low-cost lunches. Life was very difficult. At the age of eight, my mother was sent to board in a Catholic convent school, probably because of its very low fees. She studied the Catechism and learned a smattering of French. My mother later described the miserable conditions there: meals of rice with bugs in it, no heating, and a roommate who wet her bed at night and sobbed as she dragged her heavy mattress outside every morning to air it. At the age of 13, my mother started working as a typist to add to the family income.

My parents had never left the shores of the Asian mainland. Both my sister and I were born in Shanghai and had also never been abroad. My mother, sister and I were excited over the possibility of traveling overseas on vacation, but at the same time we felt a little guilty leaving our father behind to endure the unsettled political climate that had become the norm in Shanghai.

Since 1932, Shanghailanders had watched with uneasiness the relentless encroachment on their city by the Japanese forces. Few were reassured by the pompous statement of Britain's Foreign Minister Halifax during a session of the League of Nations:

"His Majesty's Government will certainly continue to bear in mind the needs of the Chinese people."

In 1939, Shanghai was divided into four distinct parts: two foreign enclaves, the International Settlement and the French Concession, each with extra-territorial rights granted in the Treaty of Nanking that terminated the Opium War in 1842; the Chinese City Government of Greater Shanghai, which included the old walled city; and the ever-expanding Japanese-occupied areas — a springboard for further Imperial "liberation."

Resentment against Japan simmered within the Chinese population. Snipers lurking in Shanghai's narrow, dark alleys shot armed members of the Japanese Naval Landing Force. Now they no longer dared venture alone on the streets and marched in groups of three or four, carrying rifles and on constant lookout for attacks. Anti-Japanese feelings ran so high that at a special meeting, 3,000 Japanese citizens demanded their home government's protection.

The Japanese called the 1932 Sino-Japanese hostilities One-Two-Eight, since they began on January 28th. Japan had never officially declared war on China, and referred to all disturbances, assassinations, bombings and military encroachments as "police actions" or "incidents." A milestone in Japanese aggression in Shanghai occurred on August 14th, 1937. On that date, dubbed "Black Saturday" by the local population, the Japanese Garrison and Chinese troops exchanged fire, and Chinese planes attempted to bombard and sink the Japanese flagship *Idzumo*, which was docked on the Whangpoo River near the Japanese Consulate. Japanese anti-aircraft retaliated, crippling two Chinese planes and loosening the 250-lb. bombs they were carrying. Unaware of this, one Chinese pilot flew over the "neutral" International Settlement, where two of his bombs detached themselves and fell into the densely crowded streets.

A second Chinese pilot, realizing the danger of his partially detached bombs, attempted to release them over the Race Course, which appeared to be deserted. Unfortunately, he miscalculated and the bombs landed in front of a nearby entertainment center called the Great World, where free rice was being distributed to thousands of Chinese refugees. Tragically, these traumatized people had recently fled from Japanese troops in the north of the city to the relative safety of the foreign enclaves.

My father, whose offices occupied the entire second floor of the Union of Canton Building, had a grandstand view of all the bombing and fighting because his windows overlooked mile-long stretches up and down the Whangpoo River. He later described to us the charred, blackened bodies, the blood and the carnage he saw on the streets as he wended his way home.

Since many of the areas under Japanese control were separated from the International Settlement and the French Concession by streets rather than by barricades, it was often difficult to determine the lines of demarcation. Thus, it was almost impossible for the British and French police to control the surging mobs of panic-stricken Chinese.

The mobilization of the Shanghai Volunteer Corps (founded in 1853) proved to be of little help, in spite of the courage and spirited efforts of its members. Thousands of refugees slept on the sidewalks of the larger streets and in the maze of small alleyways, resting their heads on their bundled belongings and using rags and old newspapers for bedding. Police wielding thick wooden batons relentlessly tried to chase these "vagrants" from Shanghai's main thoroughfares, but the homeless always returned.

Japan's goal of gaining total economic and military power in Shanghai became obvious when large complements of "Blue Jackets" (Japanese Marines) began occupying hastily built barracks. It was then that the stream of Chinese refugees seeking the protection of the French, British and Americans reached flood-like proportions. Thus, according to the newspapers, of the 5,000 people killed on Black Saturday, most were Chinese refugees. Thousands more were wounded and eventually died. The first foreigner killed in this undeclared war in Shanghai was an Englishman educated in the United States; a score of other Westerners also perished.

Japan retaliated to the unfortunate Chinese attack on the *Idzumo* by initiating trans-Pacific raids on Shanghai and, in spite of the heroic resistance by the poorly equipped Chinese forces, succeeded in strengthening its position. On August 27, 1937, a Japanese plane swooped low over the chauffeur-driven car of British Ambassador Sir Hugh Knatchbull-Hughessen and, in total disregard of its clearly displayed Union Jack, machine-gunned the vehicle, gravely wounding the prominent diplomat. In reply to Great Britain's outraged note of protest, Tokyo grudgingly apologized some days later.

Eventually, Sir Hugh was compensated by his government for his "pain and suffering" in the line of duty. Rumor had it that the large sum of 5,000 pounds awarded him reflected not so much London's sympathy for his condition as a desire to stress to the Japanese the seriousness of their action. The day after the attack, Sir Hugh's wife and two daughters boarded the S.S. *President Hoover* and sailed with other women and children to the safety of Manila. Ironically, when the ship docked in Manila and the passengers began to disembark, the most violent earthquake since 1880 hit the Philippines!

In the early winter of 1937, the Japanese organized a "victory parade" and hoisted balloons under which dangled gigantic Chinese characters proclaiming the Japanese triumph. Then, on December 12, 1937, the Japanese sank a small U.S. river patrol boat, the *Panay* — "a black day indeed" according to Tokyo's American Ambassador Grew. Japanese-American relations deteriorated further, pushing both countries to the brink of war. As usual, the Japanese news media minimized the seriousness of the situation, claiming the attack had been a mistake and that the Japanese Navy pilots had merely been executing a mission to bomb "Chinese junks and other vessels carrying fleeing Chinese soldiers..."

When President Roosevelt sent a message to the Emperor of Japan expressing his grave concern, the Japanese attempted to settle the matter by making a formal written apology. However, different texts of this document were distributed to American newspaper correspondents and to the Japanese press: In the report to the Japanese papers, passages were deleted about the recall of the Japanese Navy Commander in charge of the action and no mention was made of the fact that official orders had been issued to the troops to "exercise the greatest caution in the future..."

By 1938, Japanese forces were entrenched in the northern (or Honkew) section of Shanghai where, unfortunately, the city's power plants and waterworks were located. Thus, the Japanese had a stranglehold on the residents of the International Settlement and the French Concession, whose daily life they could now easily disrupt by cutting off these vital utilities.

Bombings and killings continued, followed by "sincere" Japanese regrets and claims that the outrages had occurred "by mistake," "due to lack of visibility," "bad weather conditions," "wrong identification," and so forth. When one Japanese statesman declared that the rest of the world misunderstood his country's "sacred mission" in China, a British radio commentator responded:

"Japan's policy is: 'Be my brother or I'll bash your head in!'"

In May 1939, China's representative to the League of Nations, the brilliant Dr. Wellington Koo, asked the League to honor its pledge to support China by supplying financial aid to help the millions of refugees displaced by the undeclared war. The response: British and French vetoes. The "Round Sun" Japanese flag appeared in ever-larger areas of China.

On September 2, 1939, John B. Powell, the editor of the *China Weekly Review*, published a short summary of a book authored by General Kiyokatsu Sato. Its subject: the imminence of a war between the United States and Japan. The bright red jacket of the book depicted the U.S. fleet in Hawaii being sunk by the Imperial Japanese Navy and Air Force. Thus, two years before the Japanese attack on Pearl Harbor, General Sato, a well-known commentator on military affairs, published the plan to attack

Honolulu as well as Japan's ultimate goal of reaching the American mainland.

By the end of 1939, the number of official U.S. notes of protest to the Japanese government had reached 300.

Fortunate foreign passport bearers, such as the British, the Americans, the French, the Dutch and the Belgians, sat poised to return to their homeland should the situation deteriorate further. Some large firms started transferring their offices to Manila or Hong Kong and, in October 1940, the American State Department ordered the evacuation of all U.S. women and children in the Far East, as well as all males not essential to business or diplomatic missions. It was in the shadow of this cloud of uncertainty and turmoil that we planned our trip to Japan.

There had been many discussions with my father weighing the pros and cons of the situation, but my mother had another forceful argument in favor of our voyage: health and hygiene conditions in Japan were known to be far better than those in China, where many dangerous diseases were endemic. In Shanghai we were vaccinated against smallpox every three years, inoculated against typhoid every two years and against cholera every year. Most foreigners washed all their fruit and vegetables in a pink solution of potassium permanganate, boiled their water and milk and avoided eating shellfish, but dysentery was still rampant.

Before leaving Shanghai for Japan, my mother, my sister and I visited the Quarantine Service for additional shots against plague and typhus. We also had to submit to blood tests to certify that our "immunity to yellow fever had been demonstrated by the mouse protection test." At the end of the ordeal, we were handed yellow-covered, six-page booklets entitled: "INTERNATIONAL CERTIFICATE OF INOCULATION AND VACCINATION (WITH HEALTH CERTIFICATE)," stating that we were "in good health, not suffering from any contagious, chronic or disease of pernicious character including Trachoma, Leprosy and Tuberculosis." The Director of the Shanghai Health Quarantine Service personally signed this precious document. We were now cleared to enter Japan.

Chapter 2

Our cabin in the *Asahi Maru* was tiny and stuffy with a porthole so high up that we could look through it only by standing on a bunk. A sweet nausea-inducing smell permeated the steamer. Lubricant? Food? Cleaning material? Perhaps a combination of all?

The heat and poor ventilation soon drove us up to the deck where we spent almost the entire journey reclining on canvas chaises longues, fighting the misery of seasickness. At prescribed intervals, a handsome young Japanese dressed in crisp white uniform would stride up and down banging on a musical gong — a summons to meals. We paid him no heed and lay with closed eyes, sucking on lemons that my mother had wisely brought along from Shanghai. When I ventured a peek, I saw the deck railing moving up and down and, beyond it, the billowing Yellow Sea. Its color had turned from muddy brown to green as we distanced ourselves from the shores of China. Passengers walked unsteadily past us, clinging onto each other for support.

On the first evening, an officer speaking halting English approached us and handed my mother long forms to complete — some 32 items in all! We were instructed to fill in blanks stating our name, sex, age, personal description, family background (names, descriptions and occupations of parents), education, religion and other details, as well as to reply to the question: "What is your object in coming to Japan?"

My mother was reluctantly leafing through the pages with barely disguised irritation when a European gentleman of military bearing came up, clicked his heels, bowed deeply and said in Russian:

"Allow me to introduce myself: I am Captain Sergei

Sergeievich Ivanoff."

My mother replied, also in Russian, giving him our names. Captain Ivanoff then dragged a folding chair toward us, asked for permission to sit down, glanced furtively around and whispered:

"Be careful how you fill out these forms. Be sure everything is correct, exact and complete. You know the Japanese Border Police are very strict. They are the ones who control the entry of all foreigners. Your forms will be sent to Tokyo for filing."

Taken aback, we stared silently at him. He smiled in a friendly manner and offered his "humble assistance since the charming ladies are traveling alone." He also warned us to be very cautious in what we said and did in public. He told us that a national spying system had been established in Japan some nine years ago. At that time, the press published the government's demand that its citizens report any "suspicious activity" by their family, friends and neighbors.

Japanese officials were especially suspicious of foreigners, Westerners in particular. Their resentment dated back to the 1905 Russo-Japanese War, which Japan had won — its first victory over a European nation — but which had not resulted in equal status with important Western powers, such as the United States and Great Britain.

"The Japanese are most sensitive to slights and insults — whether real or imagined," our new acquaintance clarified. He described the frightening disorder in Tokyo that lasted five days when, in the summer of 1924, hostile crowds, enraged at the U.S. Exclusion Act, tore down the Stars and Stripes from the roof of the American Embassy building and ripped it into shreds. The press was in a frenzy. Newspaper articles claimed that the new U.S. immigration law was a declaration of Japan's inferiority, a "nation of coolies." Posters had been distributed throughout the larger cities — Tokyo, Osaka, Kobe, Nagasaki,

Hiroshima — attacking the United States' "intolerable insult upon Japan," and inciting the population to hate everything American. Patriotic societies were formed, urging the Japanese people to deny themselves every luxury and to prepare for battle.

"For years now," Captain Ivanoff sighed, "anti-foreign propaganda has been growing in Japan like a painful boil." Then, noting our upset expressions, he added cheerfully:

"But, don't you worry! Japan is a beautiful, beautiful country with lovely pine trees, magnificent beaches and mountains. You will enjoy your vacation. The Japanese have so many remarkable qualities, such as a sense of beauty and harmony. I am happy here, perhaps mainly because I am a White Russian and the Japanese hate the Communists as much as I do. You too, I assume, are stateless and know very well what it means when one has neither a government to defend one's interests nor a passport to give one identity. Japan offered me sanctuary so I am grateful; and personally, I would rather the Japanese occupy Manchuria than those devils, the *Bolsheviki*."

Sergei Sergeievich then left us and soon returned with a bowl of chipped ice and slices of watermelon. He instructed us to put the chilled fruit on our foreheads — a perfect remedy against headache and nausea he claimed. Whether it was the cold fruit or its fresh smell, or both, we felt some relief from our unhappy plight. We did envy our new acquaintance as he strode vigorously on the deck, inhaling the sea breeze and totally oblivious to the constant pitching and rolling of the *Asahi Maru*. When the dinner gong sounded, he left us saying the "good air" had made him very hungry!

We spent a restless night huddled on our chaises longues under rather scratchy blankets. The sun rose — coloring the entire horizon orange-pink — the breeze blew steadily, the sea remained choppy and our ship moved up and down, left and right — alas, without pause. We went down shakily to our cabin to refresh ourselves and, upon returning to the deck, found Captain Ivanoff seated on his deck chair, staring into the distance. In the brightness of the morning light, I noticed the leathery texture of his skin and guessed that he was a man who spent a great deal of time outdoors. This assumption was confirmed when he told us that horses were the great love of his life and that he managed a prominent riding school in Yokohama.

Sergei Sergeievich said:

"As you in the world know, nobody can ride as well as the Cossacks — and I am a former Cossack officer. I fled the Bolsheviks with General Gleboff, the Commander of the Far Eastern Cossack Corps.

"There were 6,000 of us, men, women, children, all packed tightly into three ships: the *Ohotsk,* named after one of the oldest Russian settlements in the Far East; the *Mongukhan,* named after Ghengis Khan's grandson; and the *Zashchitnik* (Defender). General Gleboff managed to raise 6,000 Yen for his operation — one Yen for each one of us! We left Vladivostok in October 1922 for Shanghai, not expecting to get stuck for nine months in Korea because of red tape. There our supplies dwindled so quickly that General Gleboff sent all women, children and married military men with families to Manchuria. Some eventually reached Harbin, others Hailar and Changchun. I remained on board with 850 young single Cossacks. It was tough.

"General Gleboff had two Aides: Generals Saveliev and that blackguard, Anisimov, who later disgraced his name and the White Russian Movement by going over to the Reds, along with a number of his subordinates.

"On August 7, 1923, our ships finally sailed from Korea and, after further stops and delays, reached Shanghai on September 14. We anchored in the Woosung River, proudly flying

Russian Czarist flags, but because the Consulate of the U.S.S.
R. had already been established and recognized in Shanghai,
General Gleboff was curtly ordered to leave within 48 hours.
The local authorities demanded that we immediately hand in
all arms and lower our flags. To this shameless order General
Gleboff proudly responded,

'We refuse. This is not in conformity with Russian Naval
honor.'

"After two weeks of complicated negotiations, our men were
granted shore leave in groups of 24 at a time. The local White
Russian Community — most of whom were themselves penniless — helped us rent an apartment in the French Concession.
The situation on the ships had become quite desperate and
people had begun to die of hunger and disease. Most of the first
group of officers to enter Shanghai were also in urgent need of
medical attention.

"Eventually, without requesting prior permission, our three
ships moved closer to the shore and dropped anchor in front of
the Quarantine Building on the Bund. The *Zashchitnik* and the
Ohotsk remained there for three years and four months.
Crewmembers rotated between the vessels and the rented apartment in 'Frenchtown,' as Shanghailanders called the
Concession. Fortunately for me, a wealthy Japanese businessman saw me riding at a show at the Race Course and hired me
to manage his riding school in Yokohama. I was able to leave
for Japan and escape the misery and humiliation my comrades
had to endure."

Captain Ivanoff sighed and lit a European-style Japanese ciga-
rette with an attached mouthpiece. He inhaled and said:

"Not bad at all, this tobacco. You know, in spite of their
hatred for America, the Japanese also produce American-style
cigarettes without filters. They try to export them to China, but
in spite of Japanese propaganda slogans like 'Asia for the Asi-

atics' and a 'New Order,' the Chinese won't buy them. They detest the Japanese even more than they do the colonial powers."

I had a number of stateless Russian friends in Shanghai, as did my parents, but I had never heard the story of General Gleboff, which fascinated me. The families of my friends had all fled from the Russian revolution, many coming by train and ship, first to Harbin and later southward to Shanghai. They had a very hard time at first; they spoke only Russian and could not work in their professions. As a result, some men became night-club bouncers, bodyguards or policemen, while the women eked out a living as seamstresses, cooks, manicurists, hairdressers and bar hostesses. As the years passed and the Russian immigrants learned English, some opened dress salons and fur stores, others obtained jobs in British, American and French firms or re-entered professional life as engineers, dentists, doctors, teachers, musicians, actors and artists. As the Russian's economic situation improved, their cultural life began to flourish.

In Shanghai, "White Russians" (in contrast to those with Soviet passports) were represented by the White Russian Emigrants Committee, a body created in 1926. This Committee registered all Russian immigrants in Shanghai and issued identification papers that were recognized by the Chinese Bureau of Foreign Affairs. In actual fact, the Committee fulfilled many of the functions of a consulate. At first, Russian Jews were part of the White Russian Emigrants Committee but in 1932 they formed a splinter group, the Shanghai Ashkenazi Jewish Communal Association. In 1937, the Shanghai Municipal Council officially declared this Association to be a separate, distinct body under the umbrella of the White Russian Emigrants Committee. That same year the Association was registered with the Chinese authorities and my father became its Honorary Secretary.

When we decided to travel to Japan, it was to the Shanghai

Ashkenazi Jewish Communal Association that my mother had to apply for the necessary travel documents. Our entry visas to Japan were stamped on those papers.

Chapter 3

We sailed into Nagasaki among green islands that looked like emeralds dropped by a giant fist into the sea. Japanese Tourist Class families who had boarded the *Asahi Maru* with us wearing Western-style clothing now appeared on deck in cotton summer kimono. They were home again. Sailors dropped anchor while we leaned over the railing watching a Quarantine launch draw near. Smartly uniformed officials climbed aboard our steamer; they were members of the Police Department under whose authority the Quarantine Services functioned. Slowly they circulated among the passengers, peering closely at each and every one and checking carefully vaccination and inoculation booklets to verify the validity dates of the stamps.

When we went ashore — straight to the Customs shed — we saw stevedores wearing nothing but G-strings unloading our steamer. The slightly-built men lifted incredibly heavy loads. At Customs we submitted our detailed questionnaires as well as an attached sheet listing all the books we had brought along, by title and author. Our single trunk, that contained nothing of value, was opened and each item examined. At that time Japan imposed high duties on imported watches and cameras, as they wanted to protect their own inferior products against foreign competition. The Customs official leafed slowly and with great attention through our books. All reading material entering Japan was carefully censored; possession of Communist literature or anything critical of Japan was a criminal offence.

All we carried was *David Copperfield, The Pickwick Papers, Little Women, Heidi, Hans Brinker and the Silver Skates* for my sister and me and a thick, well-worn copy of *War and Peace* for my mother. The Customs official was apparently satisfied. He smiled, revealing several gold teeth, and commented.

"Ah so ... you rike (like) curassic (classic) book."

To their surprise, some passengers did not have their luggage searched at all — the job had been done secretly aboard the *Asahi Maru*! As John Patrick wrote in 1943 in his book, *Why Japan Was Strong* :

> ...I was to discover that my baggage had already been completely examined before I left the ship, probably by special men assigned to the task during the dinner hours. I knew it because I'd swiped an ashtray... inscribed with the trademark of the Nippon Yusen Kaisha Steamship Line...No one could possibly have discovered it without removing everything from that bag. Yet the ashtray was gone, and everything in the bag had been replaced in exactly the position I had left it.

Sergei Sergeievich, who was remaining overnight in Nagasaki, insisted on accompanying "the ladies" to the railway station and hailed the first of some half-dozen taxis waiting in line. The driver wore neatly mended white gloves. He opened the doors for us with a courteous bow and expertly placed our luggage on the roof, tying it to two rails. As we drove through the city, my mother repeatedly exclaimed about the cleanliness, the lack of filthy beggars and mangy dogs, the toy-like wooden houses and the graceful Japanese people, moving about in their kimono like giant moths. Women carried babies strapped to their backs and held packages wrapped in kerchiefs. The movement on the streets was that of a gently flowing stream, far different from the lively chaos in Shanghai.

At the busy railway station, where groups of soldiers mixed with the crowds, we witnessed a painful scene: a middle-aged man with the rank of private stood motionless, like a stiff wooden puppet, while a young red-faced officer angrily upbraided him. People avoided glancing in their direction. My heart pounded loudly at this public humiliation.

Captain Ivanoff suggested that my mother buy three wooden *bento* boxes for our lunch on the train. Since our stomachs were still unsettled, he recommended the "sun flag" lunch — plain white rice with a pickled red plum in the center — which had become a popular symbol of Japanese frugality and self-sacrifice as the war in China progressed. We also purchased piping hot green tea in miniature earthen teapots whose lids were actually tiny cups. An old woman sold vanilla ice cream in flat paper-thin bamboo boxes but my mother preferred that we not eat frozen desserts for the time being. Sergei Sergeievich assured us that, in any case, we would have been disappointed with its watery and rather chalky texture. As we later learned, he was right. Still, we grew to enjoy this bland ice cream, as we did other kinds of Japanese foods, so different from anything we had ever eaten before.

After bidding a fond good-bye to our new acquaintance and thanking him over and over again, we climbed into our 2nd class coach. Japanese trains had 1st, 2nd and 3rd class compartments. The train was jammed. Men loosened their kimono and curled into uncomfortable balls, often occupying the entire double seat. Passengers searching for vacant places never disturbed them or showed the slightest sign of annoyance or impatience, quietly continuing their way down the aisle. Women cared for lively children with exemplary gentleness and loving indulgence. They smiled and nodded at us, offering us soft round buns filled with sweet bean paste, which we found delicious. The six soldiers riding in our compartment were different — silent and sullen. We chose seats as far away from them as possible. As we rolled past the pastoral, peaceful scenery, we happily anticipated a long summer holiday different from anything we had ever experienced.

Chapter 4

My mother had wisely followed the advice of her Japanese friend in Shanghai to make part of our journey by boat through the Inland Sea. This was an arm of the Sea of the Philippines that both separated and united the islands of Kyushu, Shikoku and Honshu. We feared we would be seasick again but the shimmering water proved to be calm, its surface like a mirror. There were many fishing boats and steel-muscled men — some wearing G-strings, some entirely naked — hauled in the nets with strong rhythmic movements. Among our fellow passengers were many foreigners of various nationalities. Shortly after we settled down, stewards handed out notices warning all passengers that:

"NO PHOTOGRAPHS MAY BE TAKEN OR
SKETCHES DRAWN FROM THE SHIP"

To ensure that the message was understood by all, it was written in Japanese, Chinese, German, English and French. The truth, as we later learned, was that this picturesque landscape had become a highly fortified military zone, with the guns and fortifications camouflaged in such a manner that the green wooded hills and islands appeared undisturbed. A passenger told us the story of a Swede who had been jailed "for taking photographs of a Japanese fortress" from a ship such as ours. When the Japanese police developed his film and showed him the forbidden snapshot, he could still see no sign of military fortifications. Thereupon, a Japanese police officer angrily pointed to a spot on the picture and said:

"Maybe you don't know, but here in this place is a cannon."

The Swede's camera was confiscated, and he was released after a severe warning. Needless to say, his film was not returned.

At dinner we shared a table set for four with a tall, slim gentleman who politely rose at our approach and introduced himself with a charming French accent as Paul Monnot. It turned out that his wife, Fernande Monnot, was my sister's beloved English teacher in Shanghai at the Còllege Municipal. Paul Monnot was traveling to Yokohama to visit his mother. Fernande would eventually join him there. He described his pleasant life in Japan, where he had spent some years prior to his transfer to Shanghai. He told us that most foreigners in Japan resided in a hilly section called "The Bluff," but his mother — an individualist, as most French people are inclined to be — had rented a charming bungalow with its own private beach farther down in Miyabara. (Later, during the Pacific War, the house was completely destroyed by U.S. bombs.)

Madame Monnot had opened a *Maison de Couture* in Tokyo and commuted there by train every day. She had hired 15 tailors, two cutters and a sales staff. The professionals were all Chinese residents of Japan because, according to Madame Monnot, nobody in the world (with the obvious exception of the French) was as good at dressmaking as were the Chinese. The sales staff were Japanese women who always behaved with the exquisite courtesy inherent to their nation. The store supervisor, a man named Nakagawa-San, was equally polite and deferential.

Paul Monnot glanced around, dropped his voice and murmured softly:

"You know the Japanese always spy on foreigners. I suspect the spy in my mother's business is Nakagawa-San. He is married to our cook and policemen often come around to visit her in the kitchen and ask questions, such as: "Is everything all right? Is there anything new? Who are the guests who come to this house?

"I have never seen Nakagawa-San lose his self-control, in spite of his weakness for alcohol. Ah, il aime son saké, celui-là! (Oh, he loves his *sake* [rice wine] that one!). For a long time he tried to pressure *Maman* [Mother] to dismiss her Chinese employees, by indirect but persistent insinuations. Finally, even he had to admit that there were no Japanese tailors able to comply with *Maman's* uncompromisingly high standards. She is a very strong woman and a perfectionist in her work."

Paul Monnot continued with a detailed description of his mother's business contacts and customers. Madame Monnot's best customer was Alice Grew, the wife of the much respected U.S. Ambassador, Joseph C. Grew, who had arrived in Japan in 1932. After the Pacific War broke out, he was able to return to the United States in an exchange for Japanese diplomats stationed there.

Mrs. Grew was an elegant woman of noble bearing, sensitive to the needs and feelings of others. She was well disposed toward Japan, where she had spent three very happy childhood years. The Japanese admired her impeccable behavior, esthetic appreciation and artistic talents. One of her hobbies was painting delicate Japanese scenes in watercolors. Mrs. Grew was the granddaughter of Commodore Perry who, in 1853, had opened a crack in Japan's policy of isolation by his firm and fair behavior. He had never resorted to bullying, unlike the representatives of other Western powers. As a result, the Japanese were persuaded to sign the Treaty of Kanagawa with the United States. This led to the beginning of trade between the two countries and to the opening of an American consulate in Shimoda.

Paul Monnot obviously enjoyed a good laugh and appeared to remember verbatim unintentionally funny statements made in the Tokyo English-language press. When Ambassador Grew first arrived, a newspaper stated: "The new Ambassador is accompanied by his fourth and final daughter." Newspapers also referred to Mrs. Grew as the "daughter of Commodore Perry" — which would have made her quite ancient.

Mrs. Grew soon heard about Madame Monnot's *Maison de Couture* and ordered a dress, which turned out very satisfactory indeed. Madame Monnot, for her part, was delighted with the Ambassador's gracious wife who spoke fluent and unaccented French. Since the Grews led a very active social life, mixing with the local *crème-de-la-crème* and hosting famous visitors such as Douglas Fairbanks Sr., Mrs. Woodrow Wilson and Babe Ruth, Alice Grew required many wardrobe changes. She was a punctual, polite and ever-considerate customer. When her daughter, Elsie, married the Embassy Attaché Cecil Lyon, in October 1933, Madame Monnot designed the bride's wedding dress, Mrs. Grew's attire, and that of all the ladies in the bridal party.

Soon Mrs. Grew, whose tasteful wardrobe was much acclaimed by Japan's high society, generously introduced her dressmaker to the ladies of the Japanese nobility. Orders started pouring in from such royal personages as Princess Takamatsu and Princess Chichibu. Princess Chichibu, in particular, became a good friend of Alice Grew. She had developed a liking for American cooking. The Princess loved popcorn, and organized fudge and waffle parties. She and her guests would listen to American records on the gramophone.

"Ah! — but you cannot imagine the *theatre* accompanying the delivery of dresses to members of the Imperial family!" exclaimed Monsieur Monnot before continuing:

"Nakagawa-San would order a special, luxurious silk square, in which he tenderly and artistically wrapped the box containing the clothing. Once, when Fernande was in Yokohama on a visit, she went with Nakagawa-San and my mother to deliver a tailored suit to Princess Takamatsu. They traveled by taxi and train, Nakagawa-San all the while clutching his parcel like a fragile treasure. At the Takamatsu residence,Nakagawa-San bowed deeply in front of a sentry — while the ladies remained seated in the taxi — and handed him the precious package, which the sentry then passed on to a guard inside the gate. After a very long wait, the sentry advised Nakagawa-San that the delivery had been accepted. He was jubilant.

"When it was necessary that *Maman* make a fitting personally, lengthy and detailed arrangements had to be completed long in advance. The Princess was always courteous but even my tough *Maman* never dared sit down in her presence."

Monsieur Monnot explained that, since the war in China started, noble ladies in Japan took to wearing their old kimono, in response to notices posted in the streets:

"DRESS PLAINLY AND HONOR YOUR EMPEROR"

Japanese wives accompanying their husbands abroad were also ordered never to appear in public in Western clothing. As a result, Madame Monnot lost most of her Japanese customers, of whom she had been sincerely fond.

After dinner we went for a stroll on the deck. Yellowish lights twinkled in the distance, the water lapped gently against the sides of our ship, a soft breeze ruffled our hair. As we walked, we passed a small group of young Germans. One of the girls wore her braided hair encircling her head. Displayed on her white cotton blouse was the first swastika pin I had ever seen — blood red enamel. I shuddered. Memories of the terrified Jewish refugees pouring into Shanghai quenched my high spirits.

The refugees sought sanctuary from the Nazis in our city because Shanghai was the only place in the world where neither a visa nor proof of capital were demanded. Since most arrived penniless, my father and many members of the Shanghai Jewish Community worked night and day to help the refugees survive. Their numbers eventually totaled nearly 20,000, farmore than the city could hope to absorb.

Monsieur Monnot explained that ever since November 1936, when Japan signed the Anti-Comintern Pact with Germany and Italy, the Nazis had started infiltrating Japan. Colonel Masaka Yamawaki of the Japanese General Staff, who had pushed for the alliance, was later promoted to Major General and now, in 1939, was Vice-Minister of War.

Some 1,500 Germans had been living in Tokyo, Yokohama and Kobe since the end of World War I. The majority of these had arrived as Japanese prisoners of war when Japan — then an ally of Great Britain — conquered the German enclave in Tsingtao (China).

Tsingtao had been just a small fishing village when Kaiser Wilhelm's forces seized Kiaochow Bay in 1898, supposedly in retaliation for the murder of two German missionaries by Chinese bandits. The true reason for the assault was the Kaiser's desire not to be outdone in China by the British, Americans and French. When World War I broke out, Germany had only one garrison in Tsingtao, but its gun emplacements with revolving turrets had been constructed using state-of-the-art techniques. I had visited these powerful forts many times during a summer vacation in Tsingtao in 1937. My cousins' Russian governess had taken us to see the big German cannons. They had appeared most frightening and, indeed, had helped stop the Japanese Navy from invading Tsingtao from the sea. The Japanese finally succeeded in defeating the Germans by attacking their garrison by land.

In Japan, many German prisoners of war married Japanese women, raised families, opened flourishing business and settled peacefully in their adopted country. Their quiet life was now being threatened by Nazi party members sent to "reinforce the Embassy and Consular Staff in Tokyo." German agents busied themselves preparing lists of Japanese anti-fascists and propagating the imaginary existence of a "Japanese Section of the American Communist Party." Charts, pictures, and statistics were created which subtly disseminated anti-Semitic propaganda. The Reuter's and Havas news agencies were referred to as "Semitic," as were the International League of Women, Pen, and the Rotary Club.

At the end of 1938 the German Embassy started publishing a four-page tabloid-sized newspaper, the *Deutsche Nachrichten*. This publication was distributed to all Germans free of charge. Officially, its editor was a certain W. Zederbohm, but everyone knew the person really responsible was the German Consulate's Press Attaché, who had been Hitler's chief of propaganda in Vienna before the German annexation of Austria in 1938. The *Deutsche Nachrichten* mainly reproduced comments from German and Italian fascist news agencies.

My mother listened intently to Monsieur Monnot and her expression saddened. She told him that in Shanghai, too, the Nazis' foothold was strengthening daily. Stories began appearing in the Shanghai press that 75% of the income of local industries and business establishments went to Jews. These allegations were strongly denied by John Powell in *The China Weekly Review*. He wrote that revenue statistics of the International Settlement proved that four-fifths of local taxes were paid by Chinese retail properties and industrial or large commercial interests. It was a known fact that the Nazis now occupied a suite in the Park Hotel Tower facing the Shanghai Race Course, from which they had thrown thousands of anti-Semitic leaflets printed in English.

The Chinese had never been anti-Semitic. In fact, in the 12th century the Chinese emperor had invited and welcomed a group of Jews to Kaifeng, one of the final stops on the Silk Road. During the more than six centuries of their community's existence, the Chinese authorities had never discriminated against the Jewish residents.

In Japan, too, anti-Semitism had been unknown until the Nazi propaganda grew from a thin stream into a mighty river.

Finally, the machinations of the Gestapo began to have an effect on Japanese policy. Several Jews were arrested for "spying" and thrown into prison, where they died of mistreatment and malnourishment. Many years later, I met Dr. Patrick Frank who, in 1993, had written a letter to the *Jerusalem Post* stating:

... the area (Gora) was full of Nazi officials who pointed out Jews to the Japanese police. The charge on arrest was usually spying, although where, for whom and in what circumstances was never specified. My uncle Hugo Frank died in prison from torture and starvation. The health of my maternal step-grandfather was broken by similar treatment. There were many others who met similar fates. Women were not exempt...

Chapter 5

When we arrived in Hiroshima in 1939, it was a bustling port with a population of 340,000. A military arsenal situated near its famous castle required such top secrecy that, for the past 19 years, no foreigner had been allowed to approach this popular tourist area. The reason for this ban became obvious when Hiroshima was revealed as the base of the "Ever Victorious Fifth Army" that eventually conquered Singapore. As the Pacific War developed, shiploads and trainloads of soldiers were transferred to this port and packed into boats headed for combat in South East Asia.

Although our final destination, the village of Inokuchi, was a less than two-hour bus ride from Hiroshima, my mother decided to stop over for the night in a Japanese-style inn, the delights of which her Japanese-Canadian friend had expounded in Shanghai. Besides, the favorable Yen exchange rate made the cost almost ridiculously low. One Yen was worth about U.S. 24 cents, and a room for the three of us, with snacks and breakfast thrown in, cost only six Yen a night. My mother had exchanged some money with the *Asahi Maru* purser and she was now carrying a bag full of paper notes and coins. In spite of its large volume, our moneybag was very light. Just a year before, in 1938, all one Sen (worth 100th of a Yen) copper coins had been replaced with aluminum because copper was needed for the war industry. Paper notes were printed to replace silver 50 Sen coins because silver was needed to pay for imported goods.

Our inn was set behind a small patch of garden, so cleverly landscaped that it appeared far larger than it was. Big flat stones with shiny surfaces led to its entrance. From there the garden continued and gradually transformed itself into a pebbled hall.

A streamlet gently flowed under a slender red, wooden bridge. Yellow-orange-red goldfish swam gracefully in the water, their scalloped tails waving like silk fans.

The transition from the bustling street into this oasis of whispers, softly gliding, slippered feet and rippling water filled me with sheer joy and a life-long love for the Japanese sense of harmony and beauty.

Even the long Registration Form my mother was obliged to complete failed to dampen our spirits. It was the usual: age, height, color of hair and eyes, occupation, place of birth, parents' names, parents' place, date of birth and occupations. These were followed by the prying questions "Where did you sleep last night? Where are you going tomorrow? Where will you stay next week?" — no doubt information required for those Japanese police files mentioned by Captain Ivanoff. We were later told that a special section of the police, called *Gaikika,* was charged with the responsibility of gathering and monitoring these records.

The summer day was long; it was still light after we had bathed, eaten sweet cakes and drunk the hot green tea brought on a tray to our room. We sat on large cushions on the *tatami*-matted floor. Since all three of us had restless, energetic and adventurous dispositions, the possibility of relaxing and going to sleep was not even discussed. After receiving a small map with the name and location of our inn (in case we got lost), we set out to explore our surroundings.

On a street corner we came upon a small group of Japanese women dressed in cool kimono. In their outstretched hands they held a long, six-inch wide, spotless, white cotton band. With a small bow, they requested all female passers-by to sew a stitch in red thread. My mother, sister and I readily complied. After each stitch the ladies thanked us and tied a tiny, neat knot before snipping the thread with miniature folding scissors. We later found out that these bands were called *Sen-nin-bari* — literally "1,000 people's needles" — and were regarded as a talisman against enemy bullets. Japanese soldiers would wind them around their midriffs under their uniforms.

Few soldiers believed in the magical powers of the *Sen-nin-bari* but all were comforted by the untiring devotion of their wives, mothers, sisters and relatives, who stood outside for hours and hours, regardless of weather conditions, to gather a total of 1,000 red stitches. After a soldier was killed, this same band, stained with blood, would often be returned to the families by the soldier's comrades.

When we returned to our room after our walk, the table had been removed and three futons had been placed side by side on the *tatami*. On each was a hard, cylindrical pillow and a light pastel-colored, seersucker coverlet. On a plate in one corner, a green spiral burned, its tip shining like a glow-worm in the dark. It was a mosquito repellent that emitted a rather pleasant, medicinal smell. The room felt comforting and embracing. There were no locks on the sliding doors. None were required. Burglary and theft were hardly known and the Japanese people were so discreet that nobody would ever barge into a room without gently making his or her presence known in advance.

Early next morning we walked to the railway station to buy tickets for the evening train to Inokuchi. On one of the platforms, solemn men and women dressed formally in dark kimono stood in a silent group awaiting the arrival of a train. When the train stopped, seven soldiers dressed in perfectly pressed uniforms stepped out. They wore black armbands on their sleeves and carried boxes wrapped in immaculate white cloth, supported by equally white slings hung around their necks. As the soldiers bowed and handed the boxes to the waiting people, a total hush fell upon the crowd milling around the station. These were the remains — ashes and bits of bones — of soldiers who had fallen in China, now being borne home to their families in Japan. There was no sobbing, no crying, and no expression of grief, just dignity, courtesy and self-control. The scene unwound like a silent pantomime, directed with exquisite timing.

The thin wisteria boxes with the warriors' remains would later be placed by the bereaved relatives in alcoves reserved for precious family relics. In many cases, beside the box, loving hands would place the Japanese flag, bearing the signatures of friends, teachers and relatives of the fallen soldier — a memento that had been given the soldier when he left to fight. Other items displayed might include a hurriedly sketched map of the spot where the soldier had died, the snapshots he had carried, the preliminary and final death notifications and the blood-stained *Sen-nin-bari* belt.

The Japanese also honored their dead warriors by placing a special cake in the alcove. The cake had been presented to the bereaved families in the name of the Empress as an offering to the spirit of the soldier. These treasured cakes bore the Imperial seal and were hand-pressed into molds shaped like paulownia leaves. They were baked and dried until rock-hard, carefully checked for a flawless surface and individually wrapped in white paper before being dispatched. A note was included within the parcel stating that the Empress of Japan had bestowed the gift. Later, as battles became bloody and thousands were killed, bodies were hastily cremated *en masse,* resulting in mixed bone fragments and ashes. When the war's carnage reached its height, people whispered that the boxes contained nothing but sand or earth, since there had been neither the time nor the possibility for cremation.

We left the station in subdued spirits but our mood improved as we strolled in the city and ate lunch followed by a dessert of one of Japan's famous export items to Shanghai, the canned Satsuma oranges which were grown in the area. There was also a golden sponge cake the Japanese call *kasutera,* a local version of the 16th century Portuguese *pao de Castella,* whose recipe the Japanese had slightly altered to their taste. A large loaf of *kasutera* sold for four Sen.

The streets of Hiroshima were so different from those in Shanghai. Sounds were soft, colors bright, and the Japanese padded along in their *zori* or *geta* (footwear with a thong between the large and second toe). In spite of the large number of people, the flow was somehow harmonious — a contrast to the jerky, uneven movement in Shanghai. Poverty was less visible. I thought back with sadness to the many deformed beggars on Shanghai's pavements, to the ragged, starving refugees, and to the toiling coolies with their skeletal bodies and protruding ribs. This all belonged to another world.

We came across enormous yellow waxed parasols drying in the sun; a tofu vendor who deftly cut slabs of his wares and wrapped them in green leaves for his customers; a man selling shaved ice which he spooned into glasses and over which he poured red, yellow or green syrup; and a storyteller surrounded by an entranced group of children. The storyteller spoke in a dramatic but rather singsong voice and held up a wooden frame in which he placed succeeding pictures illustrating his tales. He had stuck a bamboo pole in the earth with thickly matted straw at the top. Brightly colored popsicles shaped like roosters, pigs and flowers were poked into the straw. My mother bought one each for me and for my sister; they tasted of burnt sugar and were delicious. Everywhere we went the Japanese greeted us with friendly smiles and small bows. How was one to reconcile the Japanese love for children and their modesty and refinement with the brutality and obscenity of their military occupation in China?

In Shanghai, before our departure, increasingly frequent outrages by the Japanese authorities were shaking the

Shanghailanders out of their usual complacency. Foreign businessmen, journalists, radio broadcasters, ministers, diplomats, and officers of numerous clubs and organizations had secretly started contacting the American Information Committee led by John Powell. The Committee's aim was to inform the authorities of the United States and other Western powers on the true situation in China. Since the Chinese Post Office in Shanghai was now under tight Japanese control, members of the American Information Committee closely followed the sailing dates of U.S. ships and handed packages of material to reliable friends bound for the United States or the Philippines. These were pre-stamped with U.S. postage, to be mailed at the first opportunity. Thus they hoped to circumvent Japanese censorship and confiscation. Committee members also contributed mailing lists. Copies were even sent to President and Mrs. Roosevelt, to Secretary of State Cordell Hull, to each Congressman and Senator, and to every State Governor.

Only later, when he was tortured by the Japanese *Kempetai* (military police) in the infamous Bridge House in Shanghai, would John Powell find out that Japanese agents in America had managed to get hold of copies of the publications and had forwarded them to Tokyo. Fortunately, the *Kempetai* did not have a complete list of Committee members and was unable to extract it from the courageous Powell, whose spirit did not break during his barbarous ordeal. He was eventually repatriated to the United States in a prisoner-of-war exchange and died shortly after the war as a result of the abuse he had suffered in the hands of the Japanese.

Chapter 6

When we finally arrived in Inokuchi, our taxi stopped in the gathering dusk in front of a row of two-storied houses. A soft golden light shone from oil-lamps hanging above each entrance. City ordinance had prescribed that no public funds were to be provided for street lamps. Moths and mosquitoes circled around the spheres of light.

A shriveled old woman and a younger one greeted us in front of the sliding door. Miako, the family's adopted teenage daughter, whom we had met in Shanghai — and the only person in the household who spoke English — hurried from the back of the house to welcome us. Speaking shyly in heavily accented English, she insisted on dragging our trunk up the stairs. We caught a glimpse of two small children peeking curiously from behind the adults' backs. There was a rather chubby boy and a girl whose head was shaved all around, leaving an island of shiny black hair on the top of her head like a Japanese porcelain doll. Little could we guess that the entire family, with the exception of Miako (who had returned to China), would be wiped out some years later in the Hiroshima atomic explosion.

Our room was large and practically empty. There were two wall cupboards, one for our belongings and the other for bedding. Against the wall stood a diminutive, toy-like dresser that enchanted my sister with its two deep drawers and a long narrow mirror. In the middle of the room was a low reddish lacquered table. Just below the ceiling, big metal hooks protruded from each corner of the room.

After offering us some refreshments, the ladies pushed the table aside and unrolled our bedding on the *tatami*. The grandmother handed us a bundled mosquito net and showed us how to hang its four loops, one on each corner hook, thus forming a cubical room of netting to protect us against mosquitoes and other flying insects. The mother then led us downstairs pointing out a washroom with a deep wooden bathtub, its water heated by firewood. In a shed in the yard was the toilet, a bulky wooden box with a hole in its top. The rickety door on the tiny outhouse could be closed with a flimsy hook. This was the only room we had seen that could be secured.

Feeling far from home and everything familiar, we slowly fell asleep — only to be awakened with a start by shaking, rumbling and hooting. A locomotive was rolling somewhere nearby, and the vibrations rattled our wood and paper house. Luckily, after several days we got used to the noise and slept through the din of trains transporting troops and arms to Hiroshima.

Early the next morning, we arose to loud martial music and raucous staccato-voiced announcements. Apparently the owner of the house next door was the only one on the block to own a radio, and he kindly turned it on at full volume to share it with all his neighbors. In villages such as ours radios were still a luxury. We later saw little groups of people standing outside stores, raptly listening to radios blaring triumphant war dispatches and "inspiring" music. In large cities, however, about one family in nine owned a radio.

The Japanese government had realized the propaganda value of broadcasting and attempted to maintain the illusion of ceaseless victory by strict controls on radios and on programming. All broadcasts originating outside Japan were banned. Radio stations were owned by a government monopoly. The size, power and range of all sets had to comply with minutely prescribed regulations. Illegal radios were confiscated and their owners punished. Even foreign residents removed the short-wave coils from their radios to avoid trouble with the authorities. There was no advertising. To cover expenses, the Bureau of Communications collected a monthly fee on every radio in the country; registration and licensing were compulsory.

As the war in China progressed and military control tightened, radio entertainment programs disappeared almost entirely and were replaced with propaganda. The Japanese radio network spread throughout the islands. Stations were set up in each district, and by the time we had arrived in 1939, there was no region in the country that was not reached by government broadcasts.

That first morning in Inokuchi we could hardly wait to explore the village. In contrast to the martial broadcasts, the scene on the streets was one of tranquility. People dressed in bright kimono clattered along in wooden clogs. Children crouched quietly on the ground, playing jacks with small cloth bean-filled bags, some of which had tiny golden bells that tinkled ever so softly when flung in the air. Open-front shops neatly and tastefully displayed a variety of goods: candy, biscuits, dishes, towels and clothing. Everyone stared at us in a friendly, hospitable manner, bowing slightly in greeting. We smiled shyly in return. Later, we too learned to bow back. In a fruit store we bought large purple figs and round flat pink peaches, the like of which I had never before encountered (and finally saw again half a century later in Northern Spain). Mother bought tiny balloons filled with delicious bean paste. My sister and I imitated other children on the street by squeezing the paste into our mouths through a small opening. White bread was available, but neither cheese nor butter were to be found. (In fact, when dairy products were introduced after the Pacific War, most Japanese were at first revolted by them — especially by the smell of cheese.) My mother bought vegetables, fruit, sardines and rice biscuits. The air was clear. A gentle breeze blew. We felt free and happy.

When we returned home, our Japanese family was eating its mid-day meal. The rice was served by the grandmother, dressed only in a brownish skirt, her pendulous empty breasts dangling as she moved. My sister and I rushed upstairs, unable to restrain our giggles. As time went by we got used to the old lady's summer outfit and did not have to choke back our laughter.

In the afternoon, we put our woolen bathing suits on under our sundresses and strolled down the hill to the nearby beach. We carried towels, crispy rice biscuits, fruit and soft drinks. In the village, we had discovered a refreshing, milky white liquid sold in green glass bottles with round marble stoppers. It became our favorite treat, but not our mother's. She was not quite as adaptable to Japanese food as we were.

"There is nothing like Chinese food!" she would declare. Sometimes she spoke longingly of the variety of pastries available in Shanghai: the scrumptious horns filled with chocolate from Tchakalians, the Armenian bakery, the *petits fours* from the French Confiserie Marcel, the American pie-a-la mode at the Foreign Y.M.C.A., the Russian specialties of the Renaissance Restaurant.

The pale beige, sandy shore was almost deserted. We walked the entire length of the bay looking for shells and shiny stones. Little crabs ran away as we advanced. Some distance away there was a small island on which grew a cluster of trees. Two young Japanese were swimming towards it with quick, vigorous strokes. Admiring their virile grace, my sister and I splashed around self-consciously in clumsy frog-like manner, while our mother — who was always terrified of the sea — paddled like a puppy, her head raised far above the shallow water, spluttering and uttering little cries as she swam.

After a while we sat down on a rock and stared at the breaking waves while deeply inhaling the sea air. The Japanese swimmers returned to the shore and, after a short deliberation, slowly approached us — no doubt surprised to see foreigners and perceiving a rare opportunity to practice English.

"You English? American?" one asked.

"No," mother answered. "We Russian. We live Shanghai."

They appeared relieved at her reply. The two boys, Yorifumi and Isao, were students. Apparently, they had been studying English at school for a number of years, but our conversation was very halting. Sometimes we all resorted to writing words in the sand because we could not understand each other's pronunciation.

My sister asked if boys and girls go to school together in Japan. Yorifumi replied that they did so only until the third grade. In the next class they were separated; boys were taught only by male teachers, while girls had females.

Not to be left out of the conversation, Isao said:

"We read about William Tell. He shoot apple on son head. Son like Japanese boy. Not afraid die."

It was not surprising that neither Yorifumi nor Isao had ever had the occasion to speak to foreigners. They both came from Hiroshima, where the number of foreign residents could be counted on the fingers of one hand. In fact, according to a 1938 census, only 6,500 foreigners lived in all of Japan.

The breeze grew stronger. The sun was slowly sinking and the sky turned pink. It was time to go home. We said good-bye to the students and reluctantly left the beach.

Chapter 7

As we came in, Miako came running towards us and handed us a long-awaited letter from my father in Shanghai. The delay, no doubt, had been caused by Japanese censorship. My father informed us, in his beautiful cursive handwriting, that Shanghai was sweltering in heat and humidity. The temperature sometimes reached 104 degrees. Every night he went to bed wet with perspiration and woke up just as wet; there were no electric fans in our home. My father said he missed us and promised to try his utmost to get two weeks off to visit us in Japan. From that moment on, I never gave up hope that he would indeed one day arrive and every night I lit a tiny oil lamp at our window so he would not miss our house when he came. Alas, he never did.

I am sure that the main reason for my father's remaining in China was not his office work but his strong commitment to easing the plight of the Jewish refugees who were pouring into Shanghai in ever-increasing numbers. In fact, before we left for Japan, the International Settlement and French Concession authorities were beginning to grumble about the continuous stream of penniless newcomers who, they claimed, would disrupt the city's already shaky economy by competing for ever-diminishing jobs.

By the time World War II broke out all transportation from Europe had ceased. Fortunately, by then some 20,000 Jewish refugees had arrived in Shanghai from Germany, Austria, Czechoslovakia, Hungary, Lithuania and Poland. Why Shanghai? Until the attack on Pearl Harbor, on December 8 (Pacific time), 1941, only Shanghai's gates remained fully open to Jews fleeing an almost certain death in their own countries.

Before our departure, my father had told us that he was confident that we, as Jews, would most probably be well-treated by the Japanese authorities because an American Jew, Jacob Henry Schiff, had helped their country financially some 35 years earlier during the Russo-Japanese War. Gratitude was inherent in the Japanese code of behavior, my father said. They would never forget a good turn.

Jacob Schiff came from a family of rabbis in the Jewish Quarter of Frankfurt. Every house there had its own identification plate — in his family's case a ship — hence the German surname Schiff. (The neighboring house bore the design of a red shield, from which the famous Rothschild name was derived.)

Schiff was a small but tough, muscular man — the result of strenuous bicycle riding. He immigrated to the United States where, in 1875, he married the daughter of the prominent financier Salomon Loeb. Soon he became a partner in the internationally renowned investment firm Kuhn, Loeb & Company and then the leader of New York's German Jewish Community. One obsessive thought, however, relentlessly pursued him: the fate of the Jews in Russia, who were being decimated by the forces of Czar Nicholas II. In fact, the Czar's anti-Semitism ran so deep that he called all objects of his scorn (including the Japanese!) *Zhidy* (a derogatory Russian term for Jews).

When the Russo-Japanese War broke out in 1904, Japan was in desperate need of funds for arms and equipment, and Baron Korekijo Takahashi was dispatched to New York to seek loans. At a dinner with prominent financiers, the Baron met Jacob Schiff. This was a most fortunate encounter for Japan because of Schiff's conviction that "the enemy of my enemy is my friend."

Schiff's hatred for the Czar had reached a peak the preceding year, after the dreadful April 6, 1903 Kishinev pogrom. In Kishinev, the capital of Bessarabia, a Russian boy had been found murdered and mutilated, a crime to which his uncle eventually confessed. Nevertheless, the Russian authorities used this heinous crime as a pretext for a wave of anti-Semitic terror. Hundreds of handbills were printed in the office of Kishinev's only — and rabidly anti-Semitic — newspaper, the *Bessarabitz*, demanding the blood of Jews in retaliation for the "ritual murder of an innocent Christian boy." As a result, 1,500 Jewish businesses were looted and destroyed, 45 Jews killed and 92 wounded or crippled. Horror stories of unspeakable atrocities against Jews — disembowelment, bashing of babies' brains, rape and mutilation of women — reached Europe and America. Indifferent to worldwide protests, the Czar instigated yet other pogroms throughout his realm, including one more in Kishinev in 1905.

Jacob Schiff took an instant liking to the courteous and cultured Baron Takahashi, with whom he was to develop a true friendship. In the winter of 1904, using all his financial clout and negotiating skills, Schiff succeeded in underwriting a Japanese bond issue of 200 million dollars. When Schiff and his wife visited Japan in 1906, Baron Takahashi arranged for the couple to attend a private luncheon with the Emperor at the Meiji Palace, an unprecedented event. Moreover, the Japanese government awarded Schiff the "Order of the Rising Sun," the highest honor Japan could confer on a foreigner. A year later, when Baron Takahashi sent his beloved daughter to study in the United States, he entrusted her to the Schiff family, with whom she lived for almost three years.

Jacob Henry Schiff died in 1920. His immeasurable contribution to Japan's first victory over a European power ultimately affected Japan's attitude towards all Jews. Even in the heat of the Russo-Japanese War, the Japanese gave Russian Jewish captives preferential treatment and the Japanese Ambassador in Washington assured American Jewry that "special friendship of the highest degree would be extended to Jewish prisoners."

One famous prisoner was the Zionist leader Joseph Trumpeldor, who lost his arm in the fighting around Port Arthur. During his yearlong incarceration in Japan, Trumpeldor was given complete access to books, freedom to establish libraries and to organize classes. Trumpeldor later settled in Palestine and was killed in the defense of a Jewish Settlement in Upper Galilee in 1920 — the same year that Jacob Schiff died.

After dinner Miako asked if we would like to go to the cinema with her. I agreed but my mother and sister decided to stay at home and read. We walked in silence through the tranquil village. A gentle breeze blew, amber lights shone above house entrances, and here and there women swept their front paths with rhythmic, soothing swooshes of their twig brooms. The only other sounds were the gentle warning tinkle of bicycle bells.

The movie house was nothing like our luxurious cinemas in Shanghai, with their uniformed ushers, comfortable seats, and vendors walking through the aisles selling candied popcorn and ice cream before the lights went out. We paid three Sen per ticket, then removed our clogs, which attendants neatly placed on shelves. We slipped into thin slippers, entered a large hall and sat on the *tatami* floor. A shabby black curtain hung above the stage over the screen. The walls of the hall were decorated with patriotic posters. Some were splashed with Japanese slogans, some with crude drawings of chained Chinese whipped by a cruel "Uncle Sam" and others depicted happy Chinese families in a flowering landscape against a background of Chinese and Japanese flags.

A newsreel opened the program. Bayonet-armed Imperial Marines marched vigorously behind a Rising Sun standard-bearer, tractors drawing artillery rolled to loud cries of "Banzai! Banzai!" and Japanese soldiers ran over a bridge somewhere in China, as corpses of Chinese soldiers lay strewn on the banks of the creek. Not a single dead Japanese was shown. In the last newsreel a horse waiting to be shod stood beside a military mobile smithy, a cellular shaped, futuristic-looking vehicle with a built-in forge and portable lights. Miako told me that the Japanese army needed horses and that private citizens willingly donated them. Later that summer I saw two soldiers enter a farmer's shed in our village and emerge pulling a horse by a rope tied to its halter. Sometimes, I would come upon several horses being led away by the military. By the end of 1939, the military had requisitioned the country's 600,000 horses.

The main feature, "Five Scouts," depicted with realism and sensitivity the grim experience of Japanese soldiers in Northern China. Later it came to be considered one of the best of the early war films made in Japan. In 1939, the Japanese Home Ministry became worried about the popular reaction to this film and toward the end of the summer started enforcing stringent new regulations. All movies had to begin by showing "persons ready to serve patriotically" setting off enthusiastically to war. Movies focused on sacrifice to the war effort and depicted set codes of behavior and heroism. Once a month free admission to cinemas was organized for families whose sons were away at war. On this day exactly at noon, everyone in every movie house in Japan had to bow for a minute of compulsory prayer and meditation. The cinema had become yet another propaganda weapon.

In China, under the pressure of Japanese domination, the Chinese were not free to produce films reflecting their true feelings. One indirect attempt was the 1939 movie "Hua Mulan Joins the Army." Its star was the popular actress Chen Yunsan. The Chinese legend of Hua Mulan dated back to the Tang Dynasty (6th century A.D.). It tells the story of a young woman who pretended to be a man and successfully led Chinese troops to victory over the northern invaders. Then as now, China was in distress. During the Japanese occupation, more than ever, the Chinese yearned for a patriotic symbol to lift the spirits of its people. "Hua Mulan" opened in Shanghai's International Settlement at the Astor Cinema, which showed first-run films in Mandarin. It broke all box office records and played for months to packed houses.

When I came home from the movies, my mother and sister were fast asleep. I crept under the huge mosquito net, undressed in the dark and lay a long time thinking. The trains rumbled with war material toward Hiroshima, our house quaked; then there was silence and, for me, an almost tangible fear of a conflict that I felt was no longer avoidable.

Chapter 8

Early in the morning my mother, my sister and I set off to the beach to watch the sunrise. Both my parents had the Russians' passionate love for landscapes, woods, plants and flowers. My father would rhapsodize about berry and mushroom picking, swimming in cold rivers, breathing in the pungent aroma of pines and smelling delicate lilies-of-the-valley. I could easily identify with this Russian attachment to nature and had a nostalgic longing for places in Siberia I had only seen in my imagination, through my parents' eyes. During summer vacations in the mountains with my mother, she would initiate endless climbs up difficult paths to admire "the most beautiful waterfall you have ever seen in your life." I always enjoyed the early rising, the grueling hike to some magical destination and the discovery of yet another natural wonder.

The sun rose slowly and colored the sky and surface of the waves. We sat silently on the cool damp sand watching the changing hues and brightening sky. Three naked fishermen were dragging a large net to the shore, where purple flower-shaped jellyfish mingled with the wriggling, shiny silver, yellow and pink fish. Before the Pacific War, Japan took great pride in being the top nation of the world for the quantity of fish caught, even surpassing the United States, which came second.

When the power of the military expanded in Japan, they secretly began to recruit fishermen as spies. These fearless men, hardened to the perils of the sea from an early age, were perfect agent material. Scores of fishermen were sent to operate in the seas bordering the California coast, among them naval officers masquerading as simple seamen, whose objective was to report U.S. fleet movements. These punctilious Japanese, who constantly worked on their charts and took soundings, amused naive American fishermen. Decades later, the son of a Hawaiian Japanese fisherman in World War II told me that after Pearl Harbor his father was allowed only to fish close to the Honolulu coast and not to sail into the open sea. By then the Americans had started suspecting all Japanese fishermen of being spies, which his father — a simple, uneducated man — never was.

That dawn, as we stood admiring the colorful catch of the fishermen, to my delight I saw the student, Yorifumi, approaching us. He smiled in a friendly manner, obviously pleased that we, too, had sacrificed our morning sleep to wander down to the beach. The fishermen generously offered us handfuls of sardines, which Yorifumi gathered in a cardboard box cover he found half-buried in the sand. He fetched matches and a penknife from his trousers that lay with some other clothing on a rock (he was wearing bathing trunks), cleaned the fish, gathered some twigs, made a bonfire and roasted the fresh catch. The four of us sat quietly, eating the crispy fish and admiring the changing colors of the sky and sea. Oh, how I wished that my father could have been there with us to meet gentle, thoughtful Yorifumi, hear the steady lapping of the waves and share our delicious fish!

My mother left to shop and prepare lunch, my sister joined a group of youngsters who were building an elaborate sand castle, and Yorifumi and I chatted in the shade of a large rock. I tried to speak slowly and control my usual spontaneous outbursts. When I was a teenager, I found it difficult not to blurt out what I considered true and right, a trait that often got me into trouble. Here in Japan, it very soon became clear to me that many thoughts were best withheld and that the consequences of loose talk could be very serious.

Yorifumi asked me about the curriculum at my school, about co-educational classes and relations between the girls and boys,

about teachers and their attitudes, and about the school subjects I especially enjoyed. He was surprised when I scoffed at
our weekly "Morals and Civics" classes, which nobody — including the teachers — took to heart. He said that in Japan
even elementary school pupils were taught high ideals and the
necessity to "sacrifice oneself for the Nation." There were special textbooks on *Shushin* (ethics or moral training), and these
were studied very thoroughly. The conversation went haltingly.
Yorifumi could write English far better than he could speak or
understand it, so most of the time the fine sand on the beach
served as our blackboard. Later, in the first year of the Pacific
War, all English classes were cancelled in Japan. Pupils were
not allowed to learn the language of the "enemy." All American and English songs were also banned.

In Shanghai, students in my class acted like rambunctious
teenagers, while in Japan girls my age behaved like genteel
ladies. Yorifumi was astonished that we were allowed to dress
as we pleased for school and that older girls even curled their
hair, painted their nails and sometimes wore make-up. His sister Noriko was compelled to dress for school in a bulky navy
blue middy uniform. Daily she whined "Itai! Itai" (It hurts! It
hurts!), as her mother tightly combed her hair into the two braids
required by her school's regulations. At school, Yorifumi's sister and the other girls were required to sit in two rows on *tatami*
mats, facing each other in total silence for long periods of time
to develop their patience and self-control. In my class, this
would have resulted in mad giggling, shuffling and whispering.

As to teaching methods, Noriko was obliged to carry a small
hand mirror to all her English classes so that she could watch
her mouth producing sounds unfamiliar to the Japanese ear —
sounds she was made to repeat over and over until her teacher
was satisfied. In spite of all these efforts, Yorifumi doubted if
she could say even the simplest sentence in English. He had

been luckier, since his English teacher had spent two years in the United States as a child, still spoke English rather fluently, and insisted on conversation classes.

When we tired of sitting we ran into the sea. Yorifumi taught me to float and even persuaded me to swim to the little island that lay off the coast. He said that if I got tired I could just lie on my back and float. He promised to remain by my side in case I needed help. When I demurred, confessing I was a very poor swimmer, he insisted: "If you want, you can." I did not really "want" but was ashamed to refuse; and indeed, in spite of much panting and swallowing of sea brine, I did reach the island in triumph. In the distance I saw the silhouette of a warship.

Towards noon I called my sister to go back home for lunch, and Yorifumi accompanied us up the hill. As we entered our lane, we saw our neighbor's 16-year old son climb a tall tree in their front yard and hoist a large Japanese flag. While he was up in the branches, the front door of his house slid open and his father appeared, carrying a rolled banner, which he carefully opened and hung above a ground-floor window. The scroll was made of stiff sackcloth, upon which thick black characters had been painted in bold strokes. Yorifumi explained that the flag indicated that a family member had left to fight for his country in China. The writing was the name of the young man (our neighbor's elder son), followed by a prayer for his "Eternal Success at Arms," and "Congratulations on being called to the colors." Roaming around the village, I had seen such flags and scrolls, some with black streamers. These young soldiers would never return home.

Several days earlier, I was awakened at break of day by the sound of voices. I peeked through the window to see what was happening. At the entrance of our neighbor's home stood a man I had previously seen — an official of some local importance. He handed the woman of the house what appeared in the yellowish light to be an envelope. Then both bowed, and the man mounted his bicycle and pedaled rapidly away. When I later described this scene to Yorifumi, he explained that most probably the woman had been handed her son's army induction orders. That night I wrote in my diary:

Dull gray skies and cold white streaks,
Dusky soft curved hills motionless and moody,
Dim warships frozen on the horizon,
Pines pushing to the pewter sky,
Timeless time,
Eternity,
A soul alone,
Solitude.

I blotted the ink, leaned back, and thought of my father. I missed him, his love for literature, his bursts of enthusiasm and his fury at injustice. Now I remembered one of my father's poems, "The Future," which had filled me with apprehension. In my diary I jotted down a quick translation, which did not do justice to the original:

...Here we are laughing, walking,
And smiling at some weak joke,
While somewhere in Tokyo, Berlin and Moscow
Steel has been molded into arms...
O future! I hear your footsteps,
I smell the blood and the fires.
I see the world engulfed in a wave
Of madness and horror...
Understand, we cannot wait
Till the dance of death encircles us,
We must go out in the streets and shout...
Let's give our all! To battle!
To battle for peace!

How my father admired the Chinese students, struggling for

justice against the colonial powers, against their own corrupt officials. He understood their aching desire for freedom and independence. As a Jew, he knew the meaning of persecution and discrimination. Russian universities established miniscule quotas for Jewish students, and my grandmother had spent months bribing petty officials to get him accepted.

After his arrival in Shanghai, my father had tried to eke out a living by giving Russian lessons. He was very young and had the good fortune to teach a group of idealistic young Chinese students. One of his pupils, the only woman in the group, once asked him if he would like to meet Dr. Sun Yat-sen, whom they all — including my father —idolized. My father gratefully accepted and the girl's father, an influential general, arranged a meeting.

My father's encounter with Dr. Sun Yat-sen remained a high point in his life. He was the only foreigner in the waiting room of Dr. Sun's modest villa in the French Concession. Dr. Sun entered exactly at the appointed time. His movements were unhurried and gentle; his gaze was that of a loving teacher and a friend. He spoke separately to each visitor and asked my father how long he had been in China. Awed by the presence of the man he venerated, my father murmured his empathy for the nationalist movement in China and his hopes for the future of the Chinese people. He added that he was a Jew and a Zionist and that he too longed for his own independent country. Dr. Sun responded that he had long admired the strength of the Jewish people, who had survived centuries of persecution. As to Zionist ideals, he understood them and sympathized with them.

My father would later say: "Dr. Sun Yat-sen is China's hope. The Chinese people suffer stoically, but one day they will be free to live in the way they deserve."

Chapter 9

Mother, my sister, and I went on a daylong excursion to Miyajima (Shrine Island), one of Japan's most sacred spots. We set off by bus, then transferred to an electric train for the trip to Miyajima-Guchi, where we boarded the ferry. The sea was utterly calm, its only ripples caused by our boat as it leisurely moved through the water. Most of the passengers were women and young children. Some mothers carried babies strapped to their backs. The babies seemed quiet and content. Just before reaching the island, we saw a red gate emerging from the sea, like a graceful, abstract sculpture. It was the famous *Torii*.

Stately pines, cypresses and cedars turned the island of Miyajima into a leafy sanctuary. No farming was permitted, and the cutting of trees was strictly forbidden on the island. Even today, more than sixty years later, all wood carvings sold to tourists on the island are made of imported wood. Wild deer roamed about fearlessly. One grabbed our mother's blouse at her breast and refused to let go. She tried pushing him away as she screamed in Russian,

"Durak! Durak!" (Fool! Fool!).

My sister and I burst into uncontrollable laughter, much to our mother's fury. Our hilarity only increased when a flock of pigeons deposited droppings on her head. No genteel Japanese maidens, we! My mother finally got rid of her aggressor by hitting him sharply on the head with her handbag. She refused to speak to us for a long while, until the beauty of the surrounding nature finally dissipated her anger.

As we passed close to some stables we came across a wizened old man leading a white horse. According to my mother, it was the Emperor's old steed that had been put out to pasture on the island.

When we returned on the ferry, it was again crowded with women and their children, whom they handled with gentle patience. Children, apparently, were women's only outlet for uninhibited affection in Japan. Throughout our stay that summer, I observed husbands treating their wives like virtual servants. Once, on a sweltering hot day, I went to visit one of our neighbors with a little gift from my mother, and found her kneeling on the *tatami*, dressed in a pretty komono and fanning her husband as he drank green tea, clad only in his underwear. Whenever he returned home, no matter how late at night or even at dawn, she was waiting, to greet and serve her *Dana-Sama* (Lord). My mother once told me (to my great amazement since she never spoke of such matters) that although the woman knew he had a mistress, she never wavered in her devotion. How different from the strong independent Siberian females in my family!

There is no doubt that in 1939 the status of women in Japan was truly inferior to that of men. Although women were permitted to attend political meetings, they could never join political parties or participate in the legislative process. Women working for the Department of Education were treated as mere hired employees without rank or title, and appointed only to minor positions. Women taught co-ed classes in the first three years of primary school but from then on they could instruct only girls, and were not eligible to fill professorships in public colleges and universities. Very few female principals headed primary schools and none managed public middle or high schools. Only after the end of World II did Japanese women get full legal and political equality with men.

At our train station we saw a group of women waving little Rising Sun flags with a great show of enthusiasm. They wore the large, ugly *monpei* pants that had become the symbol of

Japanese wartime frugality. Most *monpei* were made of faded old kimono material, and dressmakers had a hard time cutting them from the very narrow fabric. The women at the station were members of the local Women's Association. Their main function was to lift the morale of new recruits leaving for battle. The Imperial Military Reservist Association, a veterans' organization, strictly supervised all their activities.

The representatives of the Women's Association were soon joined by a dozen or so marching men, all of whom wore white sashes diagonally across their chests. Back home, Miako explained to me that the bold black characters written on them meant: "Congratulations on being called to serve your country!"

As fresh-faced country boys in new uniforms entered the train compartments, the entire group of women and men who had come to see them off loudly shouted in unison:

"Banzai! Banzai!"

When we returned to Inokuchi, my mother realized that she had left her father's walking stick in the train. It was a sturdy cane topped by a finely carved silver Mongolian head. Since it was one of the very few mementos she had from our grandfather (who had died in a cholera epidemic in China when she was very young), she was deeply distressed. She had taken this precious possession along to Miyajima as a matter of habit. It was my parents' custom — and that of many of their Russian friends — to carry walking sticks on every hike. They would stride along with great aplomb, their faces reflecting their serious resolve.

Late that night — it must have been well past midnight — Miako woke us up, saying that a policeman had come to the house and returned my mother's walking stick. We were astonished because we had neither reported our loss nor spoken about it to anyone. How did the police know that this object belonged to us? So they *did* follow our movements — *did* spy on us! The thought that people were constantly watching us was chilling.

Chapter 10

The money transfer my father had sent from Shanghai was delayed for unknown reasons, so my mother decided to visit the Kobe branch of his British trading firm, as our money had almost run out. My sister and I suspected yet another reason for my mother's trip was her need for the throbbing life of a large city. While we kids were enjoying every moment of our vacation swimming, exploring, playing and talking with our newfound Japanese friends, my mother must have missed adult company.

That summer she was a slim, healthy young woman, only five feet in height but with the energy of a constantly humming dynamo. To us, she was the bulwark we could lean upon, the one who overcame all obstacles — the practical but ever optimistic parent. While our intellectual and idealistic father had a somewhat pessimistic outlook, mother was always good company; she usually had a funny story to tell or a joke to repeat. Whenever I was ill in Shanghai, she would dash to my bedside for a brief visit, put her cool hand on my forehead, tell me I looked "much, much better" and dash off somewhere on some very "urgent, important business."

Indeed, there was constantly some needy person for whom my mother was helping to find lodging, a job, or medical care. At meals — to which she usually turned up late — we would suddenly be faced with total strangers, whom she had brought home to eat and who often shared our table for months at a time as non-paying guests. When the Jewish refugees started flooding into China, we never had less than three or four unknowns at our table — a fact my sister and I selfishly resented, since we longed to be alone *en famille* with our parents. By that time my father was hardly ever at home, since he, along with other members of the Russian Jewish Community, were fully involved in the struggle for the survival of the destitute European refugees.

Eventually, when the war broke out and the Japanese occupied Shanghai, my mother became the family's primary breadwinner by opening a very popular toy shop and children's clothing salon called the "Peter Pan Shop." (We used to giggle when Chinese customers would come into the shop and ask to speak to Mr. Pan — which was a common Chinese name.)

"Children are children," mother would say. "I love all children, even those of enemy nationality".

Decades later in various parts of the world, I was to encounter men and women who had adored the Peter Pan Shop. One gentleman, who had attended the all-boys St. Jeanne d'Arc school, told me that my mother had once organized a drawing and coloring competition for his class and handed out lovely games as prizes. A Korean woman, whom I met by chance in Seoul many years later, reminisced about her early years in Shanghai, saying that she had spent her happiest moments in my mother's store, and that she still treasured a small toy my mother had once given her.

There was not enough money for my sister and me to accompany mother to Kobe, so we remained behind in Inokuchi. Food was somewhat of a problem, since neither one of us had ever so much as boiled a kettle of water. In Shanghai our despotic Chinese cook reigned supreme in the kitchen — which was always off limits to pesky kids. Even my mother was not welcome, although she sometimes ventured in to check on sanitary conditions (which were never satisfactory). Her complaints would cause a loud outcry, with the cook threatening to leave, together with his wife — a meek, hard-working woman whom he terrorized and of whom we were fond. Since my mother detested housework in any form, she would quickly leave the kitchen, muttering under her breath, and would spend the next couple of days trying to disregard the loud, angry clatter of pans in the kitchen — a sign of the cook's displeasure.

My mother's *cuisine* in Inokuchi was limited to dropping huge crabs into a pot of boiling water and to frying fish in a pan. Taught by the ladies of the house, she also learned to cook rice over a *hibachi* charcoal brazier. This entailed first washing the grains in a basket and picking out the impurities. Although the tedium of the washing process tried her patience, she was ashamed not to be fastidious under the critical eyes of our Japanese hosts. In general, she resented the kitchen — a small, dark room without windows, always relegated to the back of the house.

"Japanese men don't care at all about their women, the selfish pashas!" she would say indignantly. "They think only of their own comfort and force their wives to cook in a dark corner, where they must bend over low *hibachi*. These poor women break their backs and never complain."

Fortunately, the three of us loved fruit and subsisted mainly on the sweet figs, peaches, plums and apricots available for a few cents in the village fruit stalls. During my mother's absence, the house's grandmother was to provide us with cooked rice, which we loved to e at with soya sauce and bits of yellow *daikon*, the ubiquitous pickled Japanese radish.

Mother tried, without success, to hide her excitement about the Kobe trip from us. I spitefully accused her of wanting to "get rid" of us, which she heatedly denied. My sister and I were secretly rather thrilled at being entirely on our own for the first time in our lives. There would be no one to tell us to come out of the sea because our "lips were turning blue," to forbid us to drink water after eating fruit or raw vegetables for fear of diarrhea, or to force us to rest after lunch. But the moment my mother left, an unexpected emptiness filled our hearts. The first night alone, as we lay cozily under our enormous mosquito net, I decided to entertain my sister with a scary story called *The Apple Tree,* which I had read in my father's thick book, *Tales of Mystery and Suspense.* It had thrilled me — and I hoped it would frighten my baby sister. The unfortunate result was not only her terror but also my own. We lay there together, huddled and trembling, feeling utterly forsaken.

At the time of my mother's visit, Kobe was Japan's foremost shipping port and handled a third of the country's overseas trade. Some one million people lived there. When she returned to Inokuchi, mother told us she had been surprised that, contrary to Shanghai, where reinforced concrete and brick were used, most new buildings in Kobe were flimsy wooden structures. A Russian resident of Kobe had explained that, since 1938, the Japanese government had forbidden all private use of steel and any other material required for the war effort. Mother brought back a clipping from an article by the Tokyo correspondent of the *New York Times* stating: "Iron is scarcer than gold. It is hard now to buy a frying pan. A month from now it will be impossible."

It had rained before dawn on the day mother walked to my father's branch office and the streets were muddy. Outside most buildings stood large pails of water to which were attached long-handled brushes. Before entering, most Japanese meticulously washed the dirt off their shoes.

"They are so clean!" mother said with admiration.

Kobe had become an important military center. It encompassed the huge Mitsubishi and Kawasaki dockyards for building warships, the Kobe Steel Works and a complex for the production of planes, locomotives, railway cars and engine parts. Throughout the city signs stated in English and Japanese:

"NO PHOTOGRAPHING AND NO SKETCHING."

The economic position of traders who dealt in export and

import was rapidly deteriorating. The Japanese government restricted the import of foreign goods, and exports dropped because of overseas boycotts against Japanese products. My father's British trading firm was feeling the pinch. The firm's Kobe office had been opened some fifty years earlier, and for decades business had progressed at a steady pace. Now with the onset of Japanese aggression in China, it was rapidly declining.

In Shanghai, my father's company was also having problems. After the conversion of Manchuria into Manchukuo by the Japanese, foreigners were practically barred from trading there. In addition, travel on the Yangtze River had become dangerous because of attacks by bandits, which meant that goods could not be easily moved from Shanghai to other parts of China.

The British manager in Kobe was handsome and courteous. He readily advanced my mother the sum she required and even invited her to dinner in a fancy restaurant. She regretfully declined, claiming a prior commitment, but the truth was that she had nothing suitable to wear. The manager was later transferred to Shanghai where, after the outbreak of the Pacific War, the Japanese incarcerated him in a camp for enemy nationals. At the end of the war, when the camp was liberated and we visited him, he had become a broken old man.

While my mother sat in the manager's office, the windows started to rattle and pencils rolled off the top of his desk. Startled, she jumped up, but the gentleman calmly reassured her:

"Not to worry! Only a small tremor, nothing like 1923!"

He had been in England on September 1st but had heard from Japanese staff members the story of the "Great Kanto Earthquake," which had all but destroyed both Yokohama and Tokyo. Buildings crashed, fires started, water poured from burst pipes and enormous clouds of dust darkened the skies. It was estimated that 150,000 people were killed and hundreds of thousands rendered homeless.

The Kobe Manager told my mother an interesting story, which the Japanese attributed to divine intervention. During the first violent tremors, the 48 foot tall, bronze Kamakura Buddha tilted and appeared about to fall flat on its face. Then another tremor put it back into its upright position. Not a single person within the temple grounds was so much as scratched, while thousands all around them perished.

My mother, for her part, regaled the Kobe Manager with a Shanghai story my father had once told her. The Company had started its business in Shanghai dealing in tea. One of its main customers was W. Wissotsky & Company of Moscow. Whenever any of the company's representatives visited Moscow, they would be regally entertained from breakfast until the early hours of the next day. Of course everyone hoped to be sent to Moscow!

At that time, tea for Russia was packed in strong hessian-cloth sacks and transported part of the way by camels. The camels sweated and the moisture became absorbed by the carrier bags, giving the tea leaves a special flavor. After railways were built, the company delivered its merchandise by rail — and the Russian customers started complaining about the change in the taste of their tea! They claimed its quality had deteriorated. Realizing what had happened, the company decided to pack camel hair as an extra layer close to the tea leaves. After that all complaints ceased.

Never one to let the time pass idly, my mother contacted a family she had known in Shanghai. They were Russian Jews from Vladivostok and had settled in Kobe some years ago. They greeted her with the famous Siberian hospitality for which — according to my parents — there was no equal.

The Jewish Community in Kobe was headed by the energetic, dedicated and capable Anatole Ponevejski, who had arrived in

1937 to open a textile business. Anatole's grandfather, Joseph, had been forcefully conscripted at the age of nine into the Czar's army where he served for 20 years: he was a *Nikolaevski Soldat*, the "property" of Czar Nicholas, with no personal rights. As in the case of all Jewish recruits, the Russian army made a calculated effort to sever him from his roots, to erase every vestige of Judaism from his mind.

This attempt failed. As soon as he was free, Joseph decided to recapture his past by adopting the surname Ponevejski — meaning "from Ponevesz," the town of his birth and from which he had been so cruelly torn away — and to recapture his Jewish faith. He settled in Irkutsk, Siberia, where Jews suffered less persecution than in Russia proper and brought up his sons according to strict religious precepts. His grandson, Anatole, was more secular in disposition but nevertheless, remained passionately attached to his family's traditions and Jewish identity. In due course Anatole became a businessman, left Russia for Manchuria, and eventually made his home in Kobe.

There, Ponevejski found a small colony of some 25 Ashkenazi Jews — Russians, Poles, and Balts — many of whom had arrived as refugees, fleeing from the Czars' violent anti-Semitic pogroms. In the summer of the year he arrived, Kobe became inundated after prolonged torrential rains — a veritable deluge. Ponevejski quickly took action. He pulled on high rubber boots and rounded up a group of strong Jewish men to help rescue the city's endangered residents. This deed was rewarded by an official letter of appreciation (signed by the local Chief of Police) and gained Ponevejski the respect of the Japanese population.

Ponevejski soon decided to consolidate the loosely knit Kobe Jews into a smoothly functioning unit, and within a short time the Kobe Ashkenazi Jewish Community was founded. This tiny community — of which Ponevejski was elected President —

was destined to play a historic role. As Nazi terror swept across Europe, Kobe gave temporary refuge to more than 5,000 Jewish refugees, who arrived between July 1940 and November 1941.

My mother's friends told her about Ponevejski's remarkable Japanese friend, Dr. Setsuzo Kotsuji, a Christian who had studied the Torah and the Talmud in its original Hebrew. In spite of being a Christian — a small minority in monotheistic Japan — Dr. Kotsuji was very well thought of in higher Japanese circles for his intellect and integrity. His close cooperation with Ponevejski and his successful intervention with the authorities later helped smooth the rocky paths of the Jewish refugees in Japan.

There was also a small group of Middle Eastern (Sephardi) Jews in Kobe. These Sephardis first arrived in Japan in 1858 as traders, not refugees, when several countries signed commercial treaties with Japan patterned on the one negotiated for the United States by Townsend Harris. It opened certain Japanese ports to foreign trade with conventional tariffs, and guaranteed freedom of religion and other rights. Relations between Ashkenazi and Sephardi Jews in Kobe were very cordial despite their different backgrounds and traditions.

When she returned to Inokuchi, we greeted our mother with undiluted joy. She regaled us with stories of her adventures: the wonderful Russian fish and meat *pirogi* (pies) her hostess had baked, the porcelain doll heads which she had bought and shipped to Shanghai to start her own toy business, the "lovely Japanese family" who hand-painted the faces of the heads. On the train, mysterious Japanese civilians had demanded her identification papers and asked questions as to her destination, the purpose of her visit in Japan and the estimated date of her return to China.

Mother brought us compressed paper flowers that magically

spread and "bloomed" in glasses of water, brown cakes shaped like leaves, albums with lacquer covers, and pens with curlicued glass nibs.

Chapter 11

Miako and I went for a long walk in the village. We bought tiny balloons similar to grapes, in shape and color. They were filled with a sweet jelly, which we squeezed through a hole onto our tongues. We stopped to watch children playing skillfully with tops that spun almost indefinitely, some with a humming sound, their colors blending into one another. A small crowd surrounded a street acrobat. He was lying on his back, with a boy balanced on his nose; the boy was supporting a bright yellow umbrella on the tip of his own nose. There was also a white-bearded old Korean with a herd of trained turtles that followed the commands he beat on a metal drum. They marched in line, in circles, and finally climbed onto a low table, the smaller animals using the larger ones as a bridge.

Miako told me that the Korean lived on the hill together with other Koreans who, she claimed, were "dirty and bad."

"Japanese never go there," she said haughtily. In spite of her protests, I stubbornly decided to see the Korean settlement for myself and, since she would not accompany me, climbed alone up a sandy path until I reached a dilapidated shantytown. Entire families lived in tiny ramshackle hovels made of thin wooden boards haphazardly nailed together.

The 600,000 or so Koreans who lived in Japan before the Pacific War (some of them for several generations) were not assimilated in Japanese communities. They were victims of fierce discrimination. The press and the general public, who staunchly believed that Koreans were "primitive" and "violent" by nature, automatically attributed any crime to them. Miako disdainfully described how Koreans "eat rice with red pepper and garlic from ugly metal bowls and they all smell." She said there was a large colony of Koreans in nearby Hiroshima but she had never visited them and knew nothing about them.

After the Great Kanto earthquake, thousands of Koreans were murdered by rampaging Japanese mobs because a rumor had been started that Korea was contemplating the invasion of Japan since disaster had left the country helpless. No one bothered to question how this aggression could be carried out when Korea had neither a navy nor armaments. Professor Taid O. Conroy wrote in his book, *The Menace of Japan*, that during the fierce tremors he and his wife crawled for shelter under grass mats:

"...Each one of us was given an armlet of blue thread to show we were not Koreans. An hour later the men appeared again and we were given a different colored armlet — a precaution against a person copying the color and becoming protected. Time and time again they changed the colors."

When Japan annexed Korea on August 22, 1909, the country was renamed Chosen and its capital, Seoul, became Keijo. A harsh policy of suppression of the Korean language and culture was instituted, and Japanese became the sole medium of communication and education. The Koreans made various attempts to shake off their oppressors (notably in 1919). All their efforts failed, however, and resulted in cruel punishment. In 1919, between the beginning of March and end of June, over 11,000 Koreans were flogged.

In 1937, when a Korean, Kitai Son, won the Marathon Race for Japan at the Berlin Olympic Games, the editors of the largest Korean newspaper, *Donga Ilbo*, published Son's photograph, but removed the emblem of the Rising Sun from his athlete's uniform through a special engraving process. In retribution, the Japanese police suspended the paper indefinitely. The following year, in 1938, General Minami, who had been appointed Governor General of Korea, announced that, "in response to the wishes of the majority of Koreans," they would be allowed to change their names to Japanese names. Koreans soon found that if they did not make the change, they would be unable to enroll their children in school, register marriages and deaths, or change property titles — in short, they could no longer pursue a normal life.

The year that we visited Japan, 1939, the National Service Draft Ordinance was introduced by the Japanese Government and, as a result, 1,000,000 Korean workers were reportedly brought to Japan to contribute to the war effort. All their letters home were censored. They had to copy and sign a text saying they were in good health and ready to sacrifice their life for the Emperor. Korean women were recruited as "comfort women" — in reality prostitutes — for the pleasure of the Japanese military in Manchukuo and China.

In Shanghai my best friend at school was Vera, whose father was Korean. She was a year older than I, tall for her age and slim. At school she bore her Russian mother's surname, Sorokina, probably because of the prejudice against all Asians that prevailed under colonial rule. Vera's father was not at all like the image of Koreans described by Miako. A nice looking, neat and quiet man, he always wore a dark suit and tie. He worked for decades in a fabric store, where I saw him quickly and efficiently measuring out fabrics and wrapping them for customers. When strolling with my friends along Avenue Joffre, I would always glance through the show-window into his shop. Whenever he caught sight of me, he would wave his hand and smile brightly, displaying two rows of immaculate teeth (a feature common among Koreans, which they attributed to the garlic in their pickled *kimchi*). Vera's father was very loving. Every Sunday, he strolled down Frenchtown's main artery, Avenue Joffre, arm-in-arm with his wife and daughter — something my busy parents never found the time to do.

When Vera was 11 she had a fatal accident in our school

playground while riding the *Pas-de-Geants* (Giant Steps), which consisted of four long ropes hanging down from a high wooden pole and ending in leather-covered loops. There were several *Pas-de-Geants* in the schoolyard but not enough for all the schoolgirls. We would wait in line for a turn, then slip our left leg into the loop and run rapidly around the pole before leaping in the air and being swung upward. Sometimes we would cross two ropes and one girl would dash forward, while the one whose rope was above hers would be hurled many feet skyward. It was an exciting game, but unfortunately Vera's head hit the pole and she died of concussion and hemorrhage. After that the ropes were removed forever but the poles remained, a stark reminder of her death.

Vera's funeral remained engraved in my mind. A group of girls from my class went together to the onion-domed St. Nicholas Orthodox Church in the French Concession. Vera lay in an open coffin, covered with white carnations and lilies. She looked like a beautiful statue, with slightly rouged lips and eyes. It was obvious that her body had become a shell, that the lively girl of whom I was so fond was gone forever. Her mother appeared on the verge of fainting and was supported by her husband. He was silent, but his face reflected his agony.

I never understood how people could hate entire ethnic groups, religious congregations or other minorities. The Japanese anti-Korean prejudice was, to me, as repulsive as anti-Semitism and other forms of racism.

When Miako and I returned home from our walk, my mother showed me a short letter she had received from my father, together with a clipping of a *Domei* (Japanese News Agency) dispatch, which had appeared in the China press. Since the story originated in Japan, my father had not feared the censors and mailed it to us without comment. It said in part:

Reviewing...the Japanese attitude towards foreigners,

Katsuji Debuchi said that extreme tolerance has invariably marked the Japanese attitude towards aliens at present as well as in the past. Mr. Debuchi further said no trouble based on racial prejudice occurred in Japan's history, as demonstrated by Japan's colonial administration in Taiwan and Chosen, the natives of which are treated in the same way as Japanese nationals.

Turning to China, Mr. Debuchi asserted that Japanese residents in China have been subjected to an indescribable persecution for many years, but the Chinese residents in Japan are now pursuing their business peacefully, as usual, despite the outbreak of the China Incident. The Chinese nationals in Japan had never been maltreated nor had a single one of them been molested or stoned, according to Mr. Debuchi.

In the light of these instances, Mr. Debuchi said that the attitude of the Japanese nation toward Jews must be quite clear.

In view, however, of the fact that some sectors have concerns about the Jewish problem, Mr. Debuchi asked the Foreign Minister to give a clear-cut enunciation of the Government's policy toward Jews. Endorsing Mr. Debuchi's view, the Foreign Minister stated that Japan had never discriminated against alien people, either through legislation or as a matter of fact.

In view of public attention attracted by an increasing number of Jews in the Far East, since last autumn the Government has decided on a definite policy toward Jews, according to the Foreign Minister who said this policy aims at no discrimination against Jews.

In accordance with the new policy, the Foreign Minister mandated that the Jewish residents in Japan shall be treated just like other foreign residents who are free from discrimination, while the Jews arriving in Japan shall be subject to the Immigration Law like other foreigners but will never be denied entry simply because of Jewish nationality.

Such reassurances were poor solace for the Jews. In Shanghai, Jews were growing more and more fearful of Japan's encroaching occupation of the city. Should things take a turn for the worse, holders of foreign passports could return to their home countries, but most of Shanghai's Jews were stateless Russians, Middle Easterners, or refugees from Nazi Germany. Where could they go? What country would accept them without official documentation? What would happen to the European refugees whose survival depended primarily on the transfer of funds by the Jewish Joint Distribution in New York, should this money be no longer forthcoming?

Chapter 12

My sister and I waded in the sea. The tide was high, the surface of the water still and the sky a turquoise blue. Three farm children were getting ready to climb into a boat and beckoned to us with friendly gestures to join them. We were no longer unfamiliar figures; the villagers no longer stared at us but seemed to accept our presence. The children pointed to their destination, the little offshore island now separated from the beach by the tide. All the youngsters were deeply browned by constant exposure to the sun. Their bodies were thin, hard, and probably undernourished. Beyond the hills lay their tiny one-acre farm, where a special area had been reserved for cherry blossom trees — trees that bore no fruit and had no practical value but that displayed their delicate pink blossoms — a cloud of loveliness — for a fortnight every year. How I admired these uncomplaining peasants' gentleness and appreciation for nature's beauty.

The youngsters' father and older brother were off fighting in China, and their mother, like many women I had seen in the fields, shouldered the entire burden of work. For long hours she stooped under the broiling sun, often with her latest baby strapped on her back.

How did it happen that once they put on military uniforms these same stoic, dignified Japanese farmers became the arrogant bullies we met in China? I did not know it then, but in time, to my great horror, I learned how the military transformed these gentle people into cruel killers. One of the exercises forced upon them during basic training was to bayonet, while blindfolded, helpless Chinese prisoners tied to poles. At the shout of "Charge!" the soldiers were forced to run forward and blindly knife their targets. When newly inducted peasants held back, they were kicked, beaten and insulted until they finally acquiesced. After this and other sadistic initiations, basically decent men became capable of committing other atrocities for the sake of *Yamato Daiichi* — the Yamato spirit of courage and dedication. Like most Japanese soldiers, they gradually accepted the "ideal" of sacrificing human life (another's or their own) in the name of the Emperor.

When we visited Japan that summer, we saw that life for farmers was indeed hard, and they were often deprived of basic amenities. Thus, the incentive to serve in the Japanese military went beyond patriotic zeal. In fact, when their sons were mobilized, long-suffering peasants would sometimes be relieved, hoping that at long last their boys would eat rice every day. In addition, conscripts who showed the slightest leadership talent were rapidly promoted and their proud families rewarded with special allotments.

My sister and I got into the rocking boat and, as it slid into the sea, let our hands drag in the cool water. Schools of silvery fish darted below us, and velvety seaweed floated in slow sensuous motion. When we reached the island, we climbed onto the rocks and collected odd-shaped pebbles and rather smelly dead starfish. One of the boys found a flat rock, which he threw skillfully into the sea, making it skip across the surface, producing concentric circles each time it hit.

Upon our return to the beach we found our mother waiting with a bag of fruit and biscuits, which we shared with our new friends. They must have been very hungry, but accepted the food reluctantly and only after mother's firm insistence. They ate slowly, in a refined manner and refused second helpings.

Isao, the fellow student of Yorifumi, whom we disliked, soon joined us. Almost immediately after he came up the farmer children discreetly left, no doubt feeling uncomfortable in the presence of this superior "intellectual." Isao was holding a copy of the Japanese translation of *Mein Kampf*. Being a great admirer of Hitler, Isao went regularly to see all German news-reels and claimed that Japan, like Germany, needed *Lebensraum* (living space). According to him, the British, Americans and French had been colonizing Asia for many years, and soon Japan would join Germany to break the hold of these exploiting countries, especially on China. Since he had difficulty communicating in speech, he had written down some of his ideas on ruled paper — which I assumed he carried around on the beach in the hope of meeting us.

Isao's appearance put an end to our fun, and mother turned homewards to prepare dinner. On previous occasions we had always managed, under one pretext or another, to cut short Isao's ranting against democracy — according to him the road to chaos — but he persisted in trying to talk to us, probably to improve his halting English. He never mentioned the Nazi anti-Semitic propaganda, which was perhaps a subject of no interest to him. Once, when I tried to question Yorifumi about Isao, his face turned mask-like, and I knew there was no point in pursuing the subject.

As we left we saw Isao climb up on a rock, sit down, open his book and start reading. There was a cool soft breeze ruffling our hair and pine needles crunched under our feet, but my heart was not tranquil — it pounded with fury at the young Japanese fascist.

At the entrance of our house the Japanese grandmother handed us a letter from the Russian Jewish family my mother had visited in Kobe. They informed us that they had read in the newspaper that there were new restrictions against Jewish refugees in Shanghai. According to this article, the Japanese Naval Landing Party Headquarters had publicly announced the "temporary halt to the resettlement of Jewish refugees in Hongkew," the section of the city under Japanese control. This new order would be applied starting August 21, 1939. Furthermore, the Japanese authorities had now made obligatory the registration of all European refugees already residing in Hongkew, and non-compliance would be punished.

My mother's friends also wrote that, due to developments in Europe, many foreign nationals who had left on home-leave that summer were not planning to return to Japan. There was some worry that the Canadian Academy of Kobe — a private co-educational school that the family's children attended — might not reopen. Most Jewish children went there. In fact, their parents had devised a transportation system whereby several taxis would pick up the children, deliver them to school and later bring them back home. Their concern was prescient. Later, at the start of the Pacific War, the Academy was transformed into an internment camp for "enemy nationals," i.e., the British, Americans and Dutch. "Stateless" children (mainly White Russian), and "neutral" boys and girls (the Swiss, Swedes, etc.) began to attend a new school in central Kobe, taught by English-speaking Japanese teachers.

Until 1939, Kobe's small Jewish Community had led a peaceful and pleasant life in Japan. It had its own synagogue and *shohet* (slaughterer of fowl according to *Kashrut* Jewish dietary laws) — a man very well-versed in the Jewish religion, who served as unofficial Rabbi. Although most of the Community was not really observant, all-important Jewish holy days were celebrated and the *shohet* gave private Hebrew lessons to those who wished to learn. In spite of Nazi pressure, the Japanese treated Kobe's Jews with respect, even after the outbreak of the Pacific War. For Passover, instead of rice rations the Jews were given flour for *mazot* (the traditional unleavened bread), which they baked in small portable ovens placed on *hibachi* charcoal braziers.

We were all invited to visit Kobe for a "good Russian meal" but my sister's and my pleas to travel were to no avail. I suspect my mother worried about the deteriorating world situation and was afraid to spend her limited funds.

That night I was awakened several times by the rumbling of trains moving toward Hiroshima. When I fell asleep again, a sense of impending disaster led to disturbing dreams. I crept out early to watch dawn break. The pearly pinks of the sky and the crisp air and the cool earth under my feet soon revived my youthful optimism, *joie de vivre* and happy anticipation.

After breakfast Miako suggested we go to Rakurakuen, an amusement park not far from a very good beach with white sand. My mother, always eager for a new experience, agreed and the four of us set off by electric train. Rakurakuen turned out to be a playground with all kinds of swings, ropes to climb and hang from, huge wheels within which one could stand and roll by leaning one's body sideways, and — what delighted my sister and me the most — enormous elephant slides with sloping trunks down which we swished with great speed. There were many teenagers in the park and, since much of the equipment was too large for little children, there was a separate section reserved for them.

Soon after our arrival an elderly Japanese gentleman presented himself to mother (wishing to spy? practice English? merely be friendly?) and was not to be shaken off. To our great amusement, after an hour or so he asked us if we would like to "sit down a little" — and upon our assenting, led us to the toilets! My sister and I giggled in the darkness of the toilets — dreadful smelly sheds with buzzing flies and mosquitoes and a large hole in the ground in which stood a removable bucket. We then proceeded to the beach, fortunately leaving our "guide" behind.

The sand was the color of cream, the beach long and wide and baked by the merciless sun. In several places rough canvas sacking had been thrown over parallel bamboo poles to provide shade for bathers. Miako had brought along a rolled straw mat, which she spread out in the shade near groups of jolly Japanese youngsters and their families. We all wore swimsuits under our dresses so there was no need to change, which was fortunate as no cabins were available. Mother unpacked our lunchbox, and while we ate, a man approached us pushing a cart piled high with ice and sliced red and yellow watermelon. Mother bought some for the four of us, and we were rather surprised when the vendor offered to sprinkle some salt on it.

We could hardly wait to get into the water. My mother stayed on the beach reading while my sister, Miako and I ran down to the sea. Here and there we saw black flags waving in the breeze which — to our misfortune — we did not realize were warning signals. Since the water was rather crowded with swimmers, my sister made her way in the direction of one of the flags, where there were no people. She waded out until the water reached her waist —and suddenly she disappeared completely from sight! Her head rose up a while later and, to my horror, she looked terrified and was gasping for air. I dashed towards her and grabbed at her, only to feel myself drawn deep down into a whirlpool. My whole being was aware of the danger of our situation and, determined not let my sister drown, I unsuccessfully tried to push her upwards above the waves. Clinging desperately to her, I surfaced several times to see Miako staring at us and laughing wildly. Eventually, strong arms seized us and pulled us out of the swirling waters. Two young Japanese men had saved our lives. They disappeared once we were on firm footing and we dragged ourselves towards the shore. Mother, suddenly realizing what had happened, dashed hysterically into the sea towards us.

We were both badly shaken and were furious with Miako, who had seemed indifferent, indeed even amused, by our plight. We learned much later that she had not offered her help so as not to impose upon us the burden of life-long gratitude, another aspect of Japanese ethics difficult for Westerners to comprehend. Following the same principle, our anonymous rescuers had quickly vanished.

The sea that day was calm on the surface, but below it strong currents pulled helpless swimmers into a strong undertow and out to sea. At the time of our near-fatal accident, a young Japanese boy also became a victim of the sea. His mother, dressed in a kimono, stood motionless on the beach holding a bundle of her son's clothing. She was silent and displayed no emotion. Strong Japanese men and youths, who had been alerted, swam around trying unsuccessfully to find the lost boy. My mother passionately admired the woman's stoicism and decided to await the outcome of the search. Finally, after the sun set, the boy's body was pulled ashore as his mother quietly looked on, her face expressionless. My mother, sister and I wept for her. How we wished we too could learn to behave in such a stoic, courageous, and noble manner. I remembered the Japanese saying that Yorifumi had once written down for me:

"The eyelids of a Samurai's daughter must never know moisture."

Chapter 13

The following day the weather was cool and the skies overcast, so mother decided it was an opportune time to go shopping in Hiroshima. When our electric train approached the city, my thoughts turned back to the day when I first saw it: colorful, quaint and almost unreal. I now saw Hiroshima through the eyes of one familiar with the sights and sounds of Japan. Still, an aura of mystery remained.

Hiroshima was an expanse of flat land with only one protuberance, Mt. Hiji (Hijiyama). Since the Ota River and its six tributaries generously watered the region, boating was a favorite local pastime. On the river's banks, families with picnic *bento* snacked and fishermen crouched, holding their lines with immobile patience. By 1939, Hiroshima had become one of Japan's most important military centers. Its population, the majority of whom were docile Buddhists, had grown to 340,000. They were warm and friendly, welcoming the ever-increasing stream of military men, whom they addressed as *Heitai-San* (Mr. Soldier). Indeed, when we got off our train, a group of some fifty uniformed soldiers, obviously freshly inducted country boys, were striding past, singing lustily a song whose tune I grew to love. We were to hear it over and over again that summer. I never did get a full translation of the words but was told they expressed the nostalgia of troops who were far from home (probably in Manchukuo).

The Daimaru Department Store was a four-story concrete building in which a large variety of Japanese goods were sold; most foreign imports had been totally banned by now. In a special section on the third floor space had been cordoned off for a brand-new propaganda exhibit. The walls were plastered with posters stating, as the English-speaking store manager translated for us:

"One Strength — the Japanese
Our Military Forces are Strong
Asia for the Asiatics"

A large caricature depicted Chiang Kai-shek scowling as he watched Chinese crowds cheer Japanese troops in Nanking, now the seat of a puppet government.

The centerpiece of the display was an enormous blue table-top representing the Pacific Ocean, surrounded by a brass railing around which crowds gathered. People politely made way for us to come forward and watch miniature warships put into motion by a humming clockwork underneath. Two fleets were in fierce battle, one Japanese and the other an undefined Caucasian enemy (tiny sailors with yellow hair). The fight ended with Japan's decisive victory, accompanied by a loud chorus of *"Banzai!."* A Japanese officer then addressed the onlookers, exhorting them in a barking voice to "build more ships." His address was followed by a rather scratchy recording of Japan's national anthem, based on a Japanese poem written some 1,000 years ago and set —amazingly — to the music of a foreigner, one Franz Eckert, a German music teacher employed by Japanese bands between 1879 and 1898.

There was, of course, no mention of the 1937 "rape" of Nanking. Back in Shanghai, we had read what was claimed to be the translation of a *Nichi Nichi Shimbun* report. It told of two victorious Japanese officers meeting in Nanking after the atrocities had been committed. After formal bows, they drew their swords and pointed with pride to the badly nicked edges of the long blades. One said:

"I have killed 105 — how many have you killed?"

The other replied:

"Aha-ha, I have killed 106 — so sorry!"

Propaganda was so much easier to spread in Japan than in

China. Here the literacy rate was more than 90% and almost everyone could read newspapers publicizing official versions of political and military events. In China, alas, the great majority of the population could neither read nor write and the radio was unknown in much of its vast territory. On the sidewalks of Shanghai I had often observed little tables at which sat serious looking men, usually wearing glasses — a sign of education! On the tabletop were brushes, an inkstick and inkstone, a water dropper and paper. These men were scribes, whose job it was to fill out forms, compose letters, and respond to inquiries for their illiterate clients. Some specialized in love missives, others in business correspondence, and still others in official matters.

Propaganda in China's provinces was limited to skits, songs, and picture posters. Trucks loaded with actors and singers often followed Chinese troops, reciting and singing the story of Japanese aggression and abuses. In 1937, several small Chinese film companies had produced cheap, simple propaganda films for showing in the interior of China. These, however, were only available in the Cantonese dialect, which limited their usefulness. In Japan only one language was spoken throughout all the islands — a great advantage for the dissemination of information.

As Japan's power increased in China, any attempts at spreading Chinese views were squelched. In fact there were a number of attacks on Chinese newspapers, the most notorious one on the office of the *China Press*, where the Chinese version of the English daily was being printed. Late one night six armed gangsters tried to break in, presumably to kill Chinese linotype operators and pressmen. Luckily, a watchman caught sight of the intruders and quickly slammed shut a heavy iron gate. At that very moment a policeman was passing by and heard the loud noise. He shot at the intruders and they returned fire. In the exchange, an American and a Chinese were killed and other pedestrians were wounded. It was later determined that the gunmen had been hired by local Japanese to frighten the composing and pressroom staff into leaving their jobs.

A Shanghai journalist friend of my father's once told us that from the very beginning of their China campaign, the Japanese had spread propaganda through visiting tourists, lecturers and businessmen. Their purpose was to ensure sympathy and support among the Chinese, mainly by attacking the Western powers.

My mother, sister and I wandered into the clothing department of the Daimaru Department Store, where my mother bought me a gray sweater with navy-blue piping and a red anchor embroidered on the breast pocket. My sister got dressy patent leather shoes and, for herself, my mother purchased a length of satiny black silk with tiny scattered flowers, which our Chinese tailor in Shanghai later cut into a slinky evening gown. In the toiletry section we purchased pink tooth powder in flat round metal containers.

By now we were very hungry. We went to the top-floor restaurant and ordered deep fried prawns served with steamed rice, finely chopped raw cabbage, three slices of *daikon* and a side dish of red watermelon. Wooden chopsticks in glassine bags were placed on the cleanly wiped table.

As we started eating, we heard a familiar voice say in Russian: "Ach! moi tri damochki." (Oh! my three little ladies.)

It was our shipboard acquaintance, Captain Ivanoff, who had come to Hiroshima on business. He joined us for lunch and appeared delighted to hear about Inokuchi, its friendly people and sandy beach. He remarked that we were "blooming like flowers" and again insisted that both my sister and I had grown!

Sergei Sergeievich told us that he had just had been to the Central Police Station to pick up a list of Japanese driving reguations published in English for foreigners. One of his new duties was to chauffeur important business friends of his boss, the riding school owner. He showed us the instructions, printed on poor quality paper:

Rules of the Road in English

1. At the rise of the hand policeman, stop rapidly.

2. Do not pass him or otherwise disrespect him.

3. When a passenger of the foot heave in sight, tootle the horn. Trumpet at him, melodiously at first, but if he still obstacles your passage, tootle him with vigour, express by word of mouth the warning "Hi Hi."

4. Beware the wandering horse that he shall not take fright as you pass him by. Do not explode the exhaust box at him as you pass him by. Go soothingly by.

5. Give big space to the festive dog that shall sport in the roadway.

6. Go soothingly in the grease mud, as there lurks the skid demon.

7. Avoid tanglement of dog with your wheel spokes.

8. Press the braking of the foot, as you roll around the corner to save collapse and tie up.

Captain Ivanoff said that he had had no problem obtaining a driver's license. The policeman in charge of the licensing department had even given him some free driving lessons, firmly rejecting his offer of payment. The reason for this generosity was because his boss had bought a Japanese-made vehicle, which the government encouraged. If he had purchased a foreign-made car, the granting of a driving permit would have been delayed for months.

The rain stopped and Captain Ivanoff suggested that we take a stroll through Hiroshima. Many streets and sidewalks were unpaved, muddy and uneven, but elegant Matsubara-cho (Pine

Street) did the city proud: tall trees lined the avenue, their leafy tops joining high above in a green, dense canopy. Sergei Sergeievich praised the endurance, courage and dignity of Japanese women. Indeed, they walked with graceful determination, daintily avoiding puddles and splashes of mud, often while bearing babies on their backs or carrying heavy loads. They were performing a vast range of jobs while their men were at war: conductors in trains and buses, post office clerks, street cleaners, factory workers, farmers.

Several older civilian men stood in front of a bookstore, listening to a radio blaring a popular ditty, which Captain Ivanoff translated for us:

"Punish England,

The enemy of Japan,

The enemy of justice.

Banzai for the Emperor of Japan!"

A newspaper stand quickly sold out the latest edition — probably sensational news, as evidenced by thick glaring headlines.

In a stationery store, my mother bought a fine, delicately decorated writing kit for me and a book of paper dolls for my sister. The dolls, all girls, had straight short hair and a complete Japanese wardrobe, down to hair ornaments and coin purses. I secretly looked forward to "helping" my little sister cut all this out.

In Hiroshima harbor, Captain Ivanoff pointed out the small island of Ninoshima, an Army Quarantine Center. No one could foresee that after the atomic explosion in August 1945, the military would transport to it thousands of seriously wounded civilians. These unfortunates would be left unattended on the bare floor, as all the Quarantine Center doctors had burned to death.

We parted regretfully from our Cossack friend, who promised to contact us should he ever return to our part of the country.

Mrs. Rabinovich, Rena and Alla. This photograph is from the travel documentation used by the family to travel to Japan in 1939.

A family celebration in the Rabinovich home in Shanghai. Rena's mother is second at right, her father's mother, "Babushka," at front left, Rena at fourth left, and her maternal grandmother, Katia Kriger, standing at the rear.

Rena's mother, about 1938.

Rena's father in the office.

Rena at prize-giving day at the College Municipal Français.
Each book represents an award for a different subject.

The Bund, Shanghai's waterfront.

The Bund, looking southward from the Garden Bridge.

The Cenotaph on the Bund, a memorial to the Allied dead of World War I. It was pulled down by the occupying Japanese in 1941 and the bronze figures melted down to make armaments.

British Highlanders, called "Scotties" by the Shanghailanders, marching across Garden Bridge as Japanese soldiers look on. The photo was probably taken in 1939, when the Japanese had not yet made their move into the international settlements.

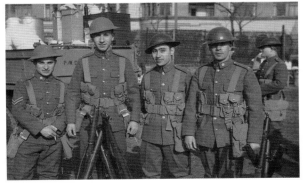

Jewish members of the Shanghai Volunteer Corps (SVC).

Paul Monnot, of Shanghai and Yokohama, walking his dog in Shanghai's suburbs.

A street in Yokohama decorated for the Emperor's coronation in 1926. (By 1939 the shop signs in English would have disappeared.)

The daughter of Paul Monnot's cook, with his dog in Yokohama.

A typical street in Kobe.

The Western aspect of Kobe.

A shopping street in Kobe. The schoolgirls are wearing the compulsory sailor tunics, the schoolboys uniforms with caps.

A ship sails from Kobe's pier. It is similar to that on which Rena's family departed.

Yorifumi and his elder sister.

Guests and staff of the Matsubara Hotel in Karatsu. On the back row, the second from the left is Rena's mother, and Rena is the second adult from the right. The handsome Japanese gentleman on the front row, far right, is the hotel manager.

View from the balcony of the family's room. Beyond the pines is the beach.

Rena and her mother by the sea. The bat motif on the straw hat is a Japanese (and Chinese) symbol of prosperity.

Revisiting the College Municipal Français in 1998 with friends (author at center).

The magnificent entry hall of the College

The former Jewish Club (now the Shanghai Music Conservatory).

The building which contained the Rabinovich apartment at No. 3, Rte. de Grouchy, Shanghai (photo by the editor, July 2001).

Chapter 14

The postman smiled at our happy reaction as he handed us a long-awaited letter from Shanghai. Father wrote that he had sent us a small parcel of books through an office colleague, who was travelling on business to Kobe: a collection of classic Russian short stories for my mother, *Heidi* for my sister, and my father's favorite Charles Dickens novel, *The Old Curiosity Shop*, for me. My father shared Russia's passion for the British writer, whose books had been serialized in newspapers throughout the world and avidly read by a multitude of fans — even in Siberia where my father grew up. He often described to me the excitement that overtook him as the stories developed, and his impatience at the frequent delays due to mail disruptions that — along with other difficulties — plagued the Russian Empire.

In his letter my father mentioned his deep concern for the plight of Jewish refugees in China. He was tormented by the Jewish Community's limited ability to aid these penniless people, as the city's military, political and economic situation was steadily deteriorating.

Enclosed in my father's letter was a short item clipped from *Jewish Life,* a publication in Harbin (Manchukuo), that illustrated one of the many difficulties facing the newcomers:

The Sad Plight of Stateless Refugees in Shanghai

The crushing minority of the Jewish refugees in Shanghai have almost no personal documents. The terms of their passports are expiring, and the German Consulate does not extend and does not exchange Jewish passports. In Shanghai itself there is no special need for passports and nobody bothers the holders of passports. But when one of the refugees has to leave Shanghai, on a business (or having found a posi-

tion outside of Shanghai), the problem of an expired passport
becomes critical. When leaving for America, Australia, or
other overseas countries, their Consuls use a special form
that replaces the passport, but it is worthless when one has to
leave for the neighbouring countries (North China,
Manchukuo, and so on...).

Among the refugees in Shanghai there are many Russian
Jews who, after the First World War, lived in Germany. There
are also many ex-war prisoners of the old Russian Army and
many Jews from formerly Russian Poland, who for the last
twenty years have lived in Austria and Germany.

The Ashkenazi Jewish Community in Shanghai renders
assistance to these formerly Russian Jews (who find themselves at present in Shanghai as German refugees) to obtain
Russian Emigrant documents. It is hoped that in this way it
will be possible to soften the plight of a certain number of
stateless refugees.

To this clipping my father added,

"One of our most difficult tasks is trying to find work for the
refugees, as few speak English and most are depressed by their
miserable living conditions. Most also suffer from ill health."

Indeed, many newcomers suffered bad reactions to compulsory inoculations, to which Shanghailanders' bodies appeared
to have become accustomed, such as those for cholera, typhoid,
and smallpox. Whereas we usually suffered nothing worse than
an inflamed arm, many refugees ran high fevers and become
really ill. It also took time for Europeans to realize that, since
nightsoil was used by the Chinese as fertilizer, one had to boil
water for at least five minutes to make it safe and carefully
wash all raw fruit and vegetables in a solution of potassium
permanganate.

My father had often expressed his deep disappointment that

democratic countries barred the entry of Jewish refugees in spite of their being fully aware of the terror in Europe. Even the United States was slow to react. Immigration officials delayed filling annual quotas from Germany until *Kristallnacht* on November 9-10, 1938, when Jews were slaughtered and their businesses and synagogues destroyed. After this outrage, America finally admitted more European immigrants — although the number in no way corresponded to the urgent need. Canada still demanded that Jewish refugees bring in sufficient capital (unavailable under Nazi laws) or be the agricultural experts that Canada needed. Unfortunately, this profession was not prevalent among Europe's Jews. Their situation was daily becoming more desperate.

After reading my father's letter, since the sun still struggled to make an appearance and patches of gray clouds hung in the sky, my mother, sister and I set out for the village instead of the beach. A group of boys were playing soldier, using sticks for guns and swords. As they fought they shouted: "Pah! Pah!" followed by "Banzai! Banzai!"

At an open stall we bought dried squid, fried peanuts and dried green peas. In a store, we came across Miako, her mother and grandmother buying canned goods to include in "comfort bags" they regularly sent to Japanese soldiers fighting in China. Miako told me that housewives in the village took time from their busy schedules to write "comfort letters" to the troops. Obviously these dedicated women knew nothing about the violence, abuses and spreading of drugs by their invading armies in China. The official Japanese explanation of the so-called "China Incident" was Japan's unselfish desire to "save the Chinese from corrupt warlords and gangsters." Propaganda stated again and again that Japan was a "true friend" of China and that their goal was "Sino-Japanese cooperation to the mutual benefit of both countries." Indeed, General Kenji Doihara, chief of the Kwantung Army's Special Service Section, proclaimed: "The Japanese Army has strictly no other intention than toenhance the prosperity of the general Chinese public."

Muriel Lester, an American nurse, wrote during her 1937 visit in Japan: "The sight of wounded soldiers returning from China caused the onlookers to wonderingly inquire what they had been doing. They were told: 'These are our noble men who have been over in China helping the people there get rid of their bandits.'"

Muriel Lester claimed that her interlocutors were dumbfounded (and, I imagine, disbelieving) when she informed them that a record was being sold in Geneva, Switzerland, in which one could hear the cries, screams and groans of the wounded civilians in Shanghai.

Unlike Muriel Lester, I never made such comments to the Japanese, or asked them any questions about the general situation or their personal feelings. Perhaps the reason was, in part, my youth and inexperience, but I think it was mainly because I instinctively realized the reluctance of the Japanese to express their inner thoughts and opinions, especially in what had become a police state.

Yorifumi never discussed the war in China, yet I felt almost by osmosis that he, the gentle lover of poetry, had no martial inclinations. When Yorifumi spoke of swords he did not refer to them as instruments of war but as revered objects. He described how they were tempered by hand, passed from father to son and considered so sacred that many men put rice paper in their mouths while examining a fine sword for fear polluting it with their breath. In the days of the Samurai, he told me, touching someone's sword without permission could lead to death. Even today, in spite of all modern firearms, soldiers carried swords. They inspired courage and stoicism.

There were so many things I could not rationalize in Japan

and so I simply absorbed them. Yorifumi attempted to explain certain concepts to me that would have been untranslatable, even for one excelling in both English and Japanese. One such was the term *kokutai*. It expressed the essence of Japan, the uniqueness of a nation ruled by a supreme leader — the Emperor — who was a descendant of the gods. Of course the Japanese government exploited this concept to its own ends. Each recruit in the Japanese armed forces was given a manual to read in which he was assured that if he died in military service he would become "one of the guarding deities of Japan" and would be specially honored in the temple. Japan had no "Tomb of the Unknown Soldier," but in Tokyo's Yasukuni Shrine every military man who had died in battle for his country was glorified — an honor worthy of every sacrifice.

Politicians also revived *Hakko Ichiu*. This was a term that Japan's first human Emperor — the Jimmu — used to describe his country's divine mission: "To bring the eight corners of the earth under the same roof." Politicians explained that *Hakko Ichiu* justified their country's expansionist policy. Japan was like a good father who would protect and guide other nations and lead them to a happy future.

Chapter 15

I spent the next day on the beach with my sister enjoying the silky sand, cool water and glowing sunshine. Towards evening, as we sat near the edge of the sea hugging our knees and listening to the slapping of the waves, several Japanese children joined us. We had seen them before on the beach and had noticed them glancing at us, but until now, they had never approached us. This time they must have been encouraged by the presence of Chiyoko, an English-speaking girl of 15 or so, who had lived in Hawaii and attended an American school there.

Chiyoko was delighted to be able to talk to two foreign girls, and her thoughts poured forth in rapid colloquial English, which no one in her group appeared to understand; they watched with expressionless faces in stony silence. Chiyoko must have been repressing her emotions for a long time for they now emerged in a flow of nostalgia, bitterness, and despair. She said that at school in Hawaii they had always been encouraged to ask questions, to think for themselves, to express ideas, while in Japan this was not accepted, in fact was dangerous.

Here in Japan, every morning at her school all the pupils trooped out to the courtyard where the Japanese flag was hoisted and the national anthem sung. Two pupils — usually class leaders — were chosen for the honor of raising the flag. They had learned to time their movements so that the flag reached the top of the pole at the last note and syllable of the national anthem. If they failed to do so they were severely reprimanded. At the school that her older brother attended, before the start of classes the boys bowed repeatedly in the direction of the Imperial Palace in Tokyo and recited by heart the long Rescript on Education, reaffirming their devotion to the Emperor and Japan. After that they sang the national anthem and, following an old tradition, replied to their headmaster's question:

"What is your sincerest ambition?" by shouting in unison:

"To die for the Emperor!"

I responded cautiously to Chiyoko's outpouring of feeling by words such as "Really;" "You don't say!" and similar bland statements. The smaller children in the group, probably bored by Chiyoko's long monologue, raced off with my sister. Two youngsters remained behind: a thin pock-marked boy (a rarity in Japan but not in China, where smallpox was endemic) and a girl aged about 13, far prettier than Chiyoko, whose broad flat face reminded me of a wooden Japanese doll. As Chiyoko spoke, the boy doodled on the sand with a long slim index finger while the girl stared into the distance. After a while Chiyoko fell silent. Was she uncomfortable and worried about her indiscretion?

In the year preceding our trip to Japan, in 1938, control on schools was tightened; all textbooks were censored, and before a publisher could obtain his ration of printing paper (wood pulp had become scarce), he had to demonstrate the "patriotic value" of a book. Moreover, lists of forbidden magazines and books were circulated to all educational centers. Teachers, students and social science research teams were strictly watched, and "student supervisors" were appointed, whose mission was to disclose illegal discussions. The supervisors sternly lectured students on desirable behavior. At the universities, a campus police force dealt with cases considered particularly difficult or dangerous.

The tradition in Japan for "proper thought" and suppression of "harmful" ideas was one of long standing: the Peace Preservation Ordinance had been established as far back as 1887, aiming to stop all political agitation. In 1911 a "Special Higher Police," commonly known as the "Thought Police," was founded. Its function was to nip in the bud "dangerous foreign

ideologies." In 1925, a Peace Preservation Law was enacted
that clearly established ideological limits on organizations and
individuals. The role of the Thought Police was widened to
seek out and silence anyone who might upset the social order.
The Diet strongly supported the new law and there was no public outcry against it. In 1926, the Ministry of Justice established
a "Thought Section" and introduced direct control over the
educational system.

In the 1930's, as Japan penetrated deeper and deeper into
China, efforts increased to brainwash the Japanese people. Spies
as well as regular police units infiltrated the country to aid the
Thought Police, who had acquired the power to investigate
anything and anyone. Agents watched individuals, unions and
associations, checked rumors, stifled "alien" ideas and promoted
"spiritual health." The summer we were in Japan, Premier
Kiichiro Hiranuma, one of the initiators of the Peace Preservation Law, spoke of a "spiritual mobilization," and called on the
Japanese people to:

"Let your hearts be as one, do your best in your respective
jobs, earnestly strive in public service and seek to repay the
Imperial benevolence."

Thus Chiyoko's outburst was most unusual.

Early the following morning, Miako tapped at our *shoji* sliding door and whispered to my mother:

"Kobayashi-San, Chiyoko's grandfather, wants to speak to
you."

I was most surprised since Miako had never before mentioned
Chiyoko's name, but then I supposed that everyone knew each
other in Inokuchi. My mother asked:

"Who is Chiyoko?" and I quickly told her that Chiyoko was
a girl who had spoken to us on the beach, adding in Russian:

"Ona mnogo govorila" (She talked a lot).

Kobayashi-San, dressed in a formal kimono, was sitting ramrod straight on a floor cushion in the downstairs family room that served as parlor/diningroom during the day and a bedroom at night. His face was dark and weathered and I assumed that earlier in life he had been engaged in fishing or agriculture. After bowing in greeting, he said:

"Wercome (welcome) Inokuchi," then turned for help to Miako who attempted, with little success, to translate further Japanese expressions of politeness. The true purpose of his visit, however, soon became obvious: to apologize for his granddaughter's "shameful behavior and lies."

My mother, to whom I had not reported Chiyoko's statements on the preceding evening, was unaware of what had transpired, but being nimble-minded and always on the alert to help people in trouble, she retorted:

"Oh, I am sure that Chiyoko didn't intend any wrong! You know how young people are! Sometimes they speak without thinking but they mean no harm! Please forgive her. She is a good girl."

How I loved her at this moment, how I appreciated her immediate and instinctive support, how proud I was of her! Hoping to mollify the grandfather, I quickly interjected that we had been watching the sun go down, that nowhere in the world were sunsets as beautiful as in Japan, and that I had not paid much attention to Chiyoko's words. Miako's grandmother then brought out some cups of steaming green tea and we all sipped in uncomfortable silence until Kobayashi-San finally rose, apologized for "bothering" us and left.

As we went down to the beach, my mother furiously told me never, *never* to encourage any talk about the situation in Japan because it endangered not only us but also the Japanese who shared their thoughts. I hardly heard her diatribe since my mind concentrated on guessing the identity of the child who had "snitched" on Chiyoko. Was it the pock-marked boy? The pretty

girl? One of the smaller children? Did they go in a group to
report on Chiyoko? How much had they understood? Tears or
rage came to my eyes and I angrily blurted out:
  "I want to go back to Shanghai! I hate all these spies!"
  I did not realize until my return to Shanghai that things were
also rapidly deteriorating there. Because of Japanese censorship,
my father dared not hint in his letters at the increasing problems.
Shanghailanders were becoming more and more aware that
Japan was planning an attack on the United States. Japanese
espionage and terror against American journalists and radio
announcers was increasing; they now hardly dared to out without bodyguards. Some, like the popular American broadcaster
Carroll Alcott, began to wear a bulletproof vest and to carry a
pistol. *The Shanghai Evening Post and Mercury*, run by the
American Randall Gould, was bombed, fortunately without any
fatalities. The State Department urged all Americans in China
to return to the United States as soon as possible.
  Later that morning, while my mother was frying fresh sardines for lunch, I sat in the front yard with Miako. She remarked
rather smugly that Kobayashi-San was head of the Neighborhood Association, a position of much importance.
  Before the war in China, the Associations were composed of
volunteers who collected money for night watchmen and helped
ensure fire prevention because fire was a constant danger in a
country of wooden buildings and open charcoal burners. Later
the volunteers' responsibilities began to include sanitation,
public health, pilgrimages to shrines and Shinto ceremonies
and, eventually, patriotic support for the government. They
volunteered in government savings bonds campaigns, fixed the
amounts of "voluntary" contributions for each household, and
organized groups to shout "Banzai!" when soldiers left for the
war. Headmen personally knew all the people living in their
neighborhood and passed on to the Thought Police intimate

information about every family.

In the big cities, central control was enforced by dividing the area into *ku* (wards) that were subdivided into *cho* (8 to 10 blocks), then into 5 to 10 households, supervised by the Neighborhood Association. Thus the smallest neighborhood could be controlled, and tabs were kept not only on the actions, but also on the thoughts of each individual. A person would dutifully report to the Association's headman any suspicious remarks he or she had overheard. The headman, in turn, would forward this information to the block association, who would contact the Thought Police in the ward. In the summer of 1939, eyes were watching and ears listening all around Japan. Poor Chiyoko! We never saw her again. How guilty I felt for not having stopped her indiscreet confidences.

When we returned for lunch, Miako handed my mother an envelope — a money transfer from my father's firm in Kobe. My mother opened it upstairs in our room and said with some relief:

"Papa managed to send us more that I expected. Good! I think we should spend the rest of summer in another part of Japan. It is such a beautiful country and I want you both to see more of it."

I was taken aback. I had grown to love Inokuchi, the hills, the beach, the kind farm families, the fishermen and the village vendors who now greeted us almost with familiarity. And oh, how I would miss my friendship with Yorifumi! If only I could have understood him better. What did he think of me, of my bursts of enthusiasm, of shock, of curiosity, which I tried — probably with little success — to control? Nevertheless, the incident with Chiyoko had left a deep wound of guilt and pain within my very being.

We talked late into the night and excitedly made plans for our departure.

Chapter 16

When I told Yorifumi that we would be leaving Inokuchi, his reply was a Japanese "Ah, so-desuka?" (Is that so?). After a moment of silence, he asked:

"I have permission to write letter?"

"Of course," I replied. "I will be very happy to get news from you."

He handed me the tiny notebook he always carried around, where he carefully entered new words for his English vocabulary. He asked me to jot down my Shanghai address on a blank page.

A desolate feeling of loss suddenly overwhelmed me and brought tears to my eyes. Yorifumi represented what I loved best in Japan — beauty, restraint and kindness. Those no Thought Police could possibly destroy. It was sad that we could never speak openly, that I could never learn his inner feelings, which I sensed (or perhaps only imagined) as being tinged with an idealism similar to that of my father. Indeed, by now idealistic youth had been effectively silenced in Japan.

Educational principles, which were ultra-nationalistic in 1931, turned openly militaristic in 1937. The Education Ministry tightened control over all professors, investigated the character of each and every one of them, and government officials would walk unannounced into classes to supervise lectures. Pressure on students to display "a proper attitude" increased to such a degree that most began to avoid any discussions — perhaps even thoughts — that might bring them into conflict with the authorities. Until 1939, the faculty had appointed university officials, but this function had now been taken over by the military. At Yorifumi's university there were officers giving military training in which he was compelled to participate, since any absence was punished and three absences resulted in expulsion. Scholarships were awarded only to students who satisfied the army's requirements in the fields of ideology and physical performance.

To my regret, the hateful Isao soon joined us. He again broached his favorite subject, the "incident" in China and the wish of the Chinese people to be "saved by Japan" from "foreign aggressors." According to him, the United Kingdom, France and the United States were greedy and "exploited poor Chinese people." He claimed that these Western countries were now "going down like the sun in the evening while Japan's beautiful red sun is going up." According to Isao, Japan would "free" China and there would be a "New Order" in Asia. I had to repress a chuckle as I thought of Carroll Alcott who, in his radio broadcasts in Shanghai, always called Japan's New Order its "New Odor."

In 1938, Prime Minister Konoe had outlined the objectives of the "New Order in East Asia." His country would lead the military, economic and cultural activities of China and Manchukuo and the fight against the threat of Communism and Western Imperialism. To do this, Japan had to establish bases on mainland China. No, this was not colonization, he insisted, simply proof of Japan's generosity in sharing its superior skills with its neighbors.

Isao's attitude was more than I could bear. I mumbled some excuse and set off for home. As I climbed the hill, Yorifumi joined me and we rambled together through the woods of which I had grown so fond. There were no pine needles or dry branches on the ground. Villagers collected them for household fuel. How frugal were the Japanese people, how uncomplaining about their meager lot, how different from the arrogant military who now ruled their country! After a while we rested on a little mound, listening to the loud drone of the cicadas. They would all start singing in unison, then stop suddenly — only to spontaneously begin their choir again. Was there a cicada conductor? Suddenly I felt depressed and lonely. Life was changing too rapidly, beyond my control.

At home, a letter from my father had arrived. The season the Chinese called the "great heat" still smothered Shanghai and the humidity reached 85 percent. As usual, he had attached a newspaper clipping. (I most certainly inherited from him my life-long habit of cutting out articles.) A contributor to the *North China Daily News* had given advice on how to beat the high temperatures:

"Do not keep your belt too tight...Expose yourself to the coolness of the night air but keep your stomach covered..."

Support for Hitler was rapidly increasing in Shanghai's German colony. After their defeat in World War I, Germans had been automatically downgraded to a lower stratum of international society, below the victors, the all-powerful British, Americans, and French. Now, once again, they arrogantly reasserted themselves. The Nazis among them openly declared their loyalty to the new regime in the *Vaterland*, vaunting the might of their *Fuehrer* and intimidating those who did not share their political views. All Germans were urged to prove their patriotism by sticking together, avoiding other foreigners — and of course having no contact whatsoever with Jews.

My father worried as increasing numbers of Nazis, expelled from the United States and South America, filtered into China. Circulars with lists of businesses opened by Jewish refugees were being distributed, and all "Aryans" were ordered to boycott them. There were open threats that names and photographs of Germans who did not comply would be dispatched to Nazi headquarters in Berlin.

While these dark clouds gathered, life for the Jewish newcomers was becoming harder and harder. My father wrote that he saw a young Jewish boy on the Bund doggedly trying to sell the German refugee paper, the *Gelbe Post*. Most passers-by were Chinese and cast curious glances at him; in Shanghai, Europeans never peddled papers on the street. Fortunately, the Japanese in Shanghai did not appear to cooperate with the Nazis, nor did the Chinese, as neither the Japanese nor the Chinese had ever been anti-Semitic.

Anti-Semitism, unfortunately, did flourish among many of the White Russians. A number of them were having financial difficulties, due to Shanghai's economic and political instability and to their lack knowledge of the English language — fluency was a job requirement in any foreign company. For them, Jewish refugees were new and undesirable competitors. This situation saddened my father who, in spite of the tribulations his family had undergone in Russia, always felt nostalgia for the country where he was born and grew up. This yearning was fired by his passion for the great Russian writers like Pushkin, the thick Russian forests where he had picked mushrooms and berries, the frozen rivers where he had skated, and the many good, simple people he had encountered in old Russia.

At the Shanghai Jewish Club, my father and some others, including non-Jewish Russians, had formed the *L.H.K.* (*Literaturni Hudojstveni Krujok* or Literary Artistic Circle). My father had become very close to some White Russian writers, actors and musicians. They spoke and wrote in Russian at all their gatherings and shared many cultural interests. One of my father's closest White Russian friends donated his entire collection of 437 rare Russian books to the Shanghai Jewish Club.

The pessimistic tone of my father's letter upset us, and we went to bed early. Late that night we heard murmurs and unusual movement in our hosts' quarters and my mother went down to check if help were needed. Miako explained that the little girl had developed a very high fever and that Dr. Watanabe had been called. We had seen him before, a tall, thin man who carried a rather tattered leather bag. It was rumored that he was very learned, read German medical books and practiced medicine in Inokuchi because of a sense of local patriotism — this was where he had been born. Villagers treated him with deep respect, calling him *Sensei-San* (Honorable Teacher).

In spite of all their criticism of the West, medicine was one field in which the Japanese never missed an opportunity to learn new techniques from Westerners. I had once read that as far back as 1859, a Dutchman, Dr. Van Meerdervort, had obtained permission in Nagasaki to dissect the body of a criminal who had been executed. On that day, 45 Japanese physicians assembled to watch the procedure, which lasted from dawn until sunset. People were very appreciative and the governor issued the following proclamation:

"Considering that the body of the malefactor has been of service to medical science, and consequently to the public good, the government undertakes to provide, within twenty-four hours, honorable burial of the remains of the criminal, with the cooperation of the ministers of religion."

Alas, Dr. Watanabe's efforts were to no avail and the condition of the neighbors' little girl's did not improve. My mother sat the rest of the night on the *tatami* near the child's bedding, gently caressing her hair and singing softly, as she had done when I was little and ill:

"Kin a body, meet a body
Coming through the rye."

The child watched her through feverish eyes and seemed to enjoy the calm the foreign lady brought into the room. My sister and I went to the village and bought a coloring book for the patient, as well as a miniature box of crayons. When we returned, she seemed to be feeling much better. In the evening, the grandmother brought up to our room a big bowl of delicious noodles she had made herself. The Japanese always reciprocated for an act of kindness.

The following day the little girl was clearly recuperating. Miako told us that the grandmother believed in Chinese cures and, seeing that her grand-daughter was not improving fast enough in spite of Dr. Watanabe's efforts, bought some dried snake powder, which she brewed and forced the child to drink. As a result, the girl perspired profusely and soon afterward her temperature dropped.

The next morning before breakfast I went by myself to the beach. It was a personal farewell and an effort to quietly clear my thoughts. Isao's words about the exploitation of the Chinese people now came back to me. I knew, of course, that Japan's schemes for China were not magnanimous, that they did not intend to liberate the Chinese people but merely wished to take into their own hands the power wielded by Western countries.

Busy with my own teenage life, my school, my friends, I had never seriously thought of such matters before. At the French school that I attended, we learned nothing about China. Our curriculum was identical to that current in France — for all intents and purposes, we could be living in Paris! I had never been outside of China and now, for the first time, I realized one of the intrinsic differences between China and Japan: In Shanghai, the Chinese were not masters of their destiny, did not govern their own territory. After the British victory over China in the Opium War in 1842, foreign powers acted in concert to open the huge Chinese market to Western-manufactured goods. For centuries, the Chinese had fought against persistent attempts by the West to start trade relations, but after their defeat in 1842, they could resist no longer. China's door was violently thrust open and the Chinese were compelled to grant trade, territorial and political rights to Great Britain, France, the

United States and, later, Germany and Japan.

The greatest injustice, in Chinese eyes, was the law of extra-territoriality, which was imposed on them by outside forces. This allowed foreigners to be tried, not by Chinese courts, but by a court of their own country and under their own system of law. There were now two contiguous European areas in Shanghai: the International Settlement, run primarily by the British and Americans, and the French Concession. In these two concessions, each country had its own local administration, own court of justice, own educational system, own army and police forces. Decisions were made and carried out, not by the Chinese residents, but by the English, the Americans, and the French.

Now in Japan, for the first time in my life, I was experiencing life in a country ruled by its own people, according to their own traditions and their own wishes. I thought back with horror on the insults the Chinese people bore so stoically in Shanghai: the riverside park they were not allowed to frequent, although their taxes contributed to its upkeep, the clubs they could not enter, the jobs they would never get. Here, in Japan, the picture was radically different. Although the Japanese treated foreigners politely, often offering them a seat in a crowded bus or train, this was done as a gesture of courtesy to a visitor and not in deference to his power and superior rights. No foreigner in Japan would dream of shooing a Japanese off a park bench, nor always expect the best of everything as his due.

With a shock I realized that I had not cried out against a state of affairs wherein the foreign residents of Shanghai had the arrogance to treat their host country as a nation of subordinates, of inferiors, expected to cater to their most irrational desires. It had always seemed grossly unfair to me, but then I, too, was a second-class citizen — one step above the Chinese because I was white but well below the proud bearers of a U.S., British,

French or other European passport — because we were stateless. Although he managed a branch of a British company, my father was paid less that a British employee of lower rank and had no special privileges, no paid holidays, no memberships in clubs, no company car. The situation of the Chinese employees was worse. That was just how life was. The powerful reigned supreme.

I remembered once entering the elevator to my father's office and witnessing the elevator operator arrogantly order a well-dressed Chinese to step out and take the back elevator. The man did so immediately, but I found his expression of controlled fury hard to forget. The elevator man, Chinese himself, was simply carrying out the orders imposed by foreigners in his country.

I thought of the poor rickshaw coolies who earned insufficient pennies to keep themselves alive, not to speak of their families. How often I had seen foreigners bargaining with them after reaching their destination. A policeman (usually a Sikh or an Annamite in the pay of the relevant concession), hearing the argument, would approach, inevitably commanding the defenseless coolie to go on his way and not to create trouble.

The Shanghai Club supposedly had the longest bar in the world. According to what an Englishman told my father — who had never visited the Club — there were even rules about where you could stand at the bar. Those with senior jobs positioned themselves to the left as they went in, up near the front windows, while the more junior ones stood in the middle and towards the right, down at the dark end. Of course, no Chinese, save the servants, were allowed on the premises. Nor were they welcome at the American's Columbia Country Club. I remembered that when the famous Chinese American actress, Anna May Wong, came to Shanghai to promote her latest film, she was denied entrance to the Columbia Country Club, where she had intended to bowl. Her ethnic origin was the reason for the ban. Emily Hahn, the infamous and iconoclastic journalist, expressed publicly her indignation at the treatment of Anna May Wong. In reaction, most foreign Shanghailanders merely smiled, considering this simply another peculiarity of the flamboyant and free-spirited young American writer.

Now all these injustices loomed larger than ever in my mind. I wondered what would happen should China some day become a truly independent country, with a workforce of millions of diligent and intelligent citizens. I longed for the day to come when Yorifumi and I could discuss all these matters openly. I felt totally helpless, ignorant and worthless.

We parted tearfully from the Japanese family with whom we had shared the house in Inokuchi. We were never to see them again. They all died in the Hiroshima atomic bombing, except for Miako who had gone to Shanghai to help her father.

Chapter 17

Karatsu was a resort that boasted — and rightfully so — "seven miles of golden beaches." Our hotel, the Matsubara, stood on a pine-studded hillock overlooking the seashore. Our room faced the beach and had a long balcony where we hung our swimsuits to dry. (Our good English woolen suits remained damp for a long time – but we had only one each.) We slept on single iron beds with hard mattresses, which actually seemed rather luxurious after the futon at Inokuchi. The cost, including full board for the three of us: Seven Yen per day!

(After the war, I was back in Japan and tried to book a room at the Matsubara, but it had become an R&R center for U.S. troops and was closed to the general public.)

The Matsubara manager was an unusually handsome Japanese with satiny, lightly bronzed skin and eyebrows shaped like the wings of a bird in flight. He always wore his dark kimono with natural elegance and grace. Even beyond his attractive physical appearance, he was kind, courteous and gentle with children.

The majority of the guests were foreign women and children from Tientsin, Shanghai, Harbin and Tokyo. Their husbands, like my father, had remained behind to work. During meals the youngsters, to their unanimous joy, were placed at tables separate from the adults — who were probably just as delighted to have respite from their offspring. Each day some boys and girls would be honored by having some dishes on the menu named for them, and I still have a rather faded hotel menu featuring:

"Cordon Soup a la Alla" (my sister) and

"Fried Fish a la Ira" (a Russian diminutive of my name).

The only youngsters who sat with their parents at a table for four were two German boys: a tall blond, wavy-haired 16-year old called Otto and his younger roly-poly brother, Hans. The family never talked at meals and Hans would occasionally cast envious glances in our direction as we chattered like a flock of noisy magpies. We were not surprised that they held themselves apart. It may have been the influence of their parents, and certainly that of the German school they attended in Shanghai, the Kaiser Wilhelm Schule. Although it had once been a rather international European school, now a Nazi flag fluttered above the building and the curriculum was dictated from Berlin.

Even the German Boy Scouts had been incorporated into the German National Youth Organization, now called the *Hitler Jugend*, and no other youth organizations were permitted. Should any boy be reluctant to join, his parents were at first warned, then threatened. Like their elders, German youngsters began greeting each other with the Hitler salute. Jews no longer visited a German bakery, as all customers were now routinely greeted with a lifted, outstretched arm and a vigorous "Heil Hitler!" In Japan the German school was changing and here, too, education passed into the hands of Nazi supporters.

After the war, the Kaiser Wilhelm Schule became a U.S. Officers' Club, where I frequently danced to the strains of a big band. I was once present when a hush descended upon the ballroom: General Albert C. Wedemeyer had dropped by unexpectedly. At the time, he was Chief of Staff to General Chiang Kai-shek, and Commander of the U.S. Forces in China (from 1944-1946). But who, in that last glorious summer of 1939, could possibly have even dreamed of such an enormous shift in power?

In the afternoons a great stillness would descend upon the Matsubara. All the guests would disappear into their rooms to relax, but neither my body nor my mind ever seemed to require rest. My sister was equally impatient and we would just lie there, churning and whispering. Our mother, who was trying to doze off, would exclaim in irritation:

"Both of you are impossible! Can't you ever be quiet? Just go away — do something! But be back in time for tea!"

That was the signal we had been waiting for. We quickly struggled back into our still-damp swimsuits, ran down the stairs on tiptoe (our bedroom was on the second floor) and crossed the dining room. This was the time when the *nei-san* (maids), dressed in bright kimono, would be setting the tables for tea. They did this in total silence; one never heard the rattle of cutlery or crockery. As we passed them on our way out, one of the maids would invariably murmur:

"Choto mate kudasai. (Please wait a minute)," and hand us two perfectly shaped pears, or peaches, or a bunch of grapes wrapped in a paper napkin.

At *siesta* time, the beach would usually be deserted, the waves large and "fat," casting long strands of dark-green seaweed and amoeba-shaped jellyfish onto the shore. My sister and I would dash barefoot across the hot sand and walk along the cool edge of the water, hoping to find unusual shells and odd-shaped stones.

Occasionally we would meet another restless soul on the beach. Her name was Tamara and she also lived in Shanghai. She had come to Karatsu with her Russian mother and maiden-aunt. Both ladies were the very essence of old-fashioned propriety. I had never seen them other than modestly dressed in long skirts and high-necked blouses, usually searching anxiously for Tamara, whose adventurous temperament was not to be restrained. Tamara's father, whom we later met in Shanghai, was a rather stodgy Swiss gentleman, and I wondered how such a mischievous child could have been born to two apparently such unimaginative and tight-laced parents!

Tamara, who was slightly younger than I, differed from any

of the girls I had ever met. She was an incorrigible free spirit. The week before we arrived, she had jumped off her second-floor balcony carrying her mother's and aunt's open parasols, one in each hand, and crashed down. Fortunately she landed in some bushes and had only superficial scratches and contusions. She tried to convince my sister and me to repeat the performance with "big Japanese waxed paper umbrellas that will definitely work," but neither one of us could be talked into this risky undertaking. One evening, Tamara told us that she had once run full speed down a road in Shanghai, then flung herself backwards on the asphalt "to see how it feels" — and had broken her coccyx!

Tamara's best friend in Shanghai was a Chinese girl named Evelyn, who attended the McTyeire School for Chinese girls, founded in 1892 by American missionaries. The three famous Soong sisters (later Mmes. H.H. Kung, Chiang Kai-shek and Sun Yat-sen) had all studied there. At first all the classes were taught in English, but gradually the school became more and more Chinese in character and now Chinese was the language of instruction.

Since the bombing of Chapei (where the school was originally located) by the Japanese, many students had lost their homes and life had become very difficult for them. Since that awful day, January 28, 1932, Evelyn really hated the Japanese. They had burned down the famous Dongfang Library, resulting in the loss of all its 468,000 volumes, including the whole children's section that Evelyn so loved. Luckily, 547 rare classic volumes had earlier been moved to a safe-deposit vault in the Jincheng Bank and were saved. (Today they are in a library in Beijing.) I still remembered my father's great distress when this calamity occurred (on my sister's birthday), and how he, the passionate bibliophile, had called it "a great crime."

Evelyn loved the McTyeire School and taught Tamara (who,

in turn, taught us) the first verse of Henry Newbolt's poem, "The Best School of All," that the pupils used to recite at all celebrations at the school:

It's good to see the school we knew,
The land of youth and dream,
To greet again the rules we knew
Before we took the stream.
Though long we've missed the sight of her,
Our hearts may not forget.
We've lost the old delight of her,
We keep her honor yet.

Evelyn and her family had moved to Chungking a few months before the destructive Japanese bombing raid of May 1939, when some 5,000 people were killed. Tamara fervently hoped she was safe.

How could this serious Chinese girl have become close to ever naughty Tamara? Probably because she found her feisty and inventive nature so much fun. Indeed, Tamara seemed to make unusual friends — at least according to the prevailing standards of most of Shanghai's foreigners, who chose to socialize only with Westerners.

Tamara told us about Tomoko, a *Nisei* (second generation Japanese born in the U.S.) who lived in the same "terrace" (row of town houses) where she did. Tomoko claimed that other Japanese laughed at her "Japanese face on a Westerner's body" and considered her a freak. She was a tall, slender, well-built girl who loved sports and went to the American school, but attended Japanese classes in the afternoon. There her teacher told her all Japanese children belonged to the Emperor, had to be ready to sacrifice themselves for the sake of the Japanese Nation, and should always remember the "brave soldiers fighting to free the Chinese from slavery to the West."

In Japan, claimed her teacher, many pupils were so dedicated that they did not wear warm coats in winter, in sympathy for the cold suffered by the combat troops in Manchukuo. Many pupils refused refreshments during school outings, at the thought that Japanese soldiers in China might be going hungry. Patriotic girls meticulously polished army belt buckles and mended and cleaned uniforms, many of which were grimy with dirt and blood. They always remembered their military men's brave and noble deeds, she said — looking straight at Tomoko.

When we returned to the hotel, my mother was in Tamara's room, chatting with her aunt and mother. They were exchanging memories of the day of the infamous Shanghai bombing — dubbed "Black Saturday" — as today was the second anniversary of this catastrophe. The previous year, on August 14, 1938, the first anniversary of the bombing, Shanghai had been amazingly subdued. Newspapers published photographs of empty streets. Even Nanking Road and the Bund, usually jammed with pedestrians, were comparatively empty and all amusement centers were closed. Some stores pulled down their shutters, fearing there might be trouble. Indeed, there had been several attempts at disturbances and a few suspects had been arrested. The Settlement Police later discovered that the culprits were mainly Japanese, some of whom had worn Chinese clothing. This confirmed what many Shanghailanders believed: that incidents were often artificially created by the Japanese and used as a pretext to demand more Japanese policing of the city.

Chapter 18

I had a new friend: Eddy, an 18-year old White Russian from Tokyo. Eddy always moved, or rather shuffled, slowly but his lively and intelligent, dark eyes belied his assumed languor and indifference. He called me *"malenkaya"* (little one), making me feel delicate and fragile — which I certainly was not. I relished our outings together when he ambled along voicing his thoughts — as I had always wished Yorifumi would do. Eddy had come to Japan from Vladivostok as a small child and spoke fluent Japanese, probably because in Tokyo Westerners interacted in a friendly manner with the Japanese people — unlike in Shanghai, where most foreigners enjoyed a life totally detached from that of the Chinese.

In fact, almost the only contact many foreign children had with the Chinese was with their amah, a great number of whom had "small feetee," the tiny, crippled feet that were considered a mark of feminine beauty in China. It was painful to see them in the parks, running awkwardly after their naughty charges.

Amahs (sometimes called baby amahs) reigned supreme in the nursery, where they were totally responsible for the children. Laundry would be done by a wash amah, whose status was definitely inferior. Amah was always the decision-maker and, should additional staff be required, she would be the one to recommend one of her relatives or friends for the job. Most foreign children loved and obeyed their amahs, to whom they were often closer than to their own mothers — who were often out all day playing *mah-jong* or cards, or had various social obligations.

Our amah, Ah-Kwei, had raised several young children in our family clan. She was one of the few whose feet had not been broken by the ancient foot-binding custom. She was independent, straightforward and forceful. I could well imagine her categorically refusing to allow bandages to be wrapped ever more tightly around her feet. Ah Kwei intimidated us, but we all loved her. She hated all men, the one exception, perhaps, being my father.

Eddy claimed that he had learned the Japanese language in "self defense," since the Japanese had such difficulty speaking English (contrary to many Chinese, who appeared to "catch it on the fly"). Soon after our arrival in Inokuchi, I had begun to decipher the way the Japanese pronounced English words and to understand Yorifumi and Isao — at least I believed I did. Most foreigners, however, would wonder at the meaning of:

"Haro (hello) mai (my) nai mu (name) isu (is) ..."

It appeared that the Japanese were simply unable to use consonants in clusters or to end a word with other than a vowel. Their efforts to express themselves were further complicated by the fact that they avoided terms they judged too blunt or direct, always preferring euphemisms.

Several days after our arrival in Karatsu, Eddy asked me to go with him to Hamasaki, a nearby city, to see a movie his Tokyo friends had highly praised: "Mud and Soldiers." He promised he would whisper a translation to me. We set out by electric train, and when we arrived I was disappointed to see a rather disorderly and dirty town, with neither the charm of Inokuchi nor the majesty of Hiroshima. The theater was *tatami*-floored and the screen so high that we had to crane our necks. "Mud and Soldiers" was indeed unlike most *seisen* (Sacred War) films in that it lacked the usual strident propaganda. After the movie, we discussed the remarkable Japanese self-control. Eddy attributed this characteristic to the Samurai tradition, which allowed a man to weep only on three occasions in his entire lifetime: at his father's death, his elder son's death, and the Emperor's death. The face had to remain mask-like and tears had to be wiped from each eye with one finger only.

We wandered for a while around Hamasaki, admired its life-like statue of a bronze horse, and sat on a stone bench to eat the chopped-egg sandwiches, *kasutera* (sponge cake) and fruit that the hotel had prepared for us. As we watched uniformed men hurrying past, Eddy told me how, in 1937, the older brother of his Japanese friend had received a pink postcard from the War Office calling him into military service. He was given only three days to wind up his work and to take leave of his family and friends. At that time, an induction was treated as a celebration, but by now Eddy thought that many Japanese had lost their initial enthusiasm for "freeing China from Western exploitation."

When I mentioned Isao's statements to the contrary, Eddy retorted that perhaps people in Tokyo were more sophisticated than those in Inokuchi. Be that as it may, in 1937 popular support for the war was prevalent in Tokyo and everyone had brought his friend's brother farewell gifts: packets of dried fish, razor blades, and crisp rice cakes. On the date and time designated on the call-up postcard, a large group of reservists in military uniform would arrive at a young man's home in a truck. They waved flags and banners and sang lustily as they hoisted him up and rode away towards the induction center, joining hundreds of similar trucks all over the city, carrying newly mobilized soldiers off to war. As they rolled along the streets of Tokyo, dense crowds gathered on the sidewalks, shouting repeatedly: "Banzai!."

Later many families received the ashes (or what was claimed to be the ashes) of their dead sons. Never, never had Eddy heard of any Japanese being taken prisoner or missing in action. All Imperial soldiers were either victorious or died heroically.

The sky had turned cloudy and, as we returned home in the electric train, a heavy shower started. When we got off in

Karatsu, I was amazed to see our two smiling *nei-san* waiting for us with open umbrellas. How did they know where we had gone? When we were coming home? That we had no umbrellas? Were all our movements being followed?

I told Eddy about my grandfather's walking stick that had been returned to us in Inokuchi, and he recounted a funny story about an American lady tourist who resented the constant spying in Japan. One day when she returned unexpectedly to her hotel room, she saw a Japanese snooping around and decided to take revenge. She pretended to believe he was a hotel employee and asked him to rearrange her furniture. She said she wanted the bed under the window, the chest-of-drawers on the opposite wall and the big armchair in a different corner. In short, she made the unfortunate intruder pant and sweat as he pushed and dragged furniture around while she kept changing her mind!

At the Matsubara, a long-delayed letter had finally arrived from Shanghai. My father explained in guarded terms recent developments there — none of which were cause for optimism. The Jewish refugee situation had become critical, since on August 9th the Japanese authorities in Shanghai had made public a new policy restricting further immigration of refugees. My father did not elaborate — although he was certainly privy to much information — but included a small newspaper clipping.

My father also sent us an article printed in the English-language issue of *Nichi Nichi*. It termed my favorite radio broadcaster, Carroll Alcott, a "disturbing influence in otherwise peaceful Shanghai" and stated that the American authorities should either force Alcott off the air or make him adopt a friendlier attitude towards Japan. Alcott had infuriated the Japanese by daring to criticize their aggression in China and by refusing to be intimidated by renewed warnings, attempted kidnappings, and threats on his life.

The situation had worsened this year (1939), when Alcott began broadcasting on short-wave bands that could reach Tientsin, Peiping, Chefoo, Swatow and Tsingtao, and even distant countries such as Western Australia, New Guinea, Java, Iraq and Iran. Although the Japanese often managed to interfere with the standard band heard in Shanghai, they were not equipped to jam short-wave transmissions, and finally ordered all Imperial Navy ships cruising in areas where the American radio station XMHA was heard to undertake this mission for them. Soon Alcott began to receive hundreds of letters from irate listeners scattered all over Asia, claiming they could not hear a word he was saying!

The following year (1940), a spokesman from the Japanese Consulate in Shanghai telephoned Alcott and said he might arrange to have the interference removed if Alcott would stop attributing the jamming to the Japanese military. Alcott consented to the arrangement and it worked for a few months, only to be followed by even heavier interference.

Alcott not only spoke on the radio but also wrote and published articles. This freedom-loving American refused to gloss over the bullying tactics of the Japanese invaders. It pained him to see Chinese peasant women carrying heavy sacks of vegetables roughly handled by the Japanese sentries, standing just outside the boundaries of the International Settlement and French Concession, and forced to pay bribes. He fumed about Chinese farmers beaten — sometimes to death — for disobeying orders of the *Kempetai* (Military Police), which they had not even understood, or for rejecting the worthless Japanese Military script as payment for produce. He mocked the leaflets distributed by the Imperial Army stating that:

"If there had been no Japan in the Far East, China would have been wiped out of existence long ago. On the side of science, Japan's progress has plainly surpassed all the haughty nations of Europe and America. Japan's virtues are also superior. Aside from Japan, is there any other country good enough to be the friend of our trusted ideals?"

He laughed at slogans, such as:

"Put your trust in the Japanese Army. All good friends come from Japan."

A longing for Shanghai filled my heart, for outspoken valiant journalists, for close school friends, for Ah Kwei and, most of all, for the person I loved so much, my father.

Chapter 19

It continued raining the next day, and the hotel sent a notice to all guests that a Swedish professor from Tokyo had kindly consented to give a short lecture about *Suseki* in the afternoon. It turned out that *Suseki* was a traditional Japanese art form. Natural stones were displayed on thin ceramic trays or on wooden stands. The shape, patina, and color of the stone were important, reflecting nature's beauty and harmony. *Suseki* led to spiritual thoughts, from the complexity of life to simple basic values.

I would have liked to discuss this with Yorifumi. I missed him. I had grown fonder of him than I had realized.

The hotel guests asked the professor many questions, and the conversation extended to Japanese cultural values. The speaker ended the session by telling us the story of two Japanese carpenters who, in 1935, traveled to Stockholm to build a tea-ceremony pavilion at its Ethnographical Museum. Before their departure, the structure was put on view in Tokyo and carefully inspected by Prince and Princess Chichibu, who expressed total satisfaction. The carpenters felt highly honored and vowed to refrain completely from *sake*, for which both had a weakness, during their trip abroad. This sacrifice, they believed, would purify the mind and body. They staunchly kept their resolution during their 80-day sea voyage and 100-day stay in Sweden.

In spite of their humble backgrounds, the language barrier and the shock of a new culture, the Japanese carpenters behaved impeccably throughout, thus gaining the respect and affection of all who met them. Swedes came from all over the country to admire the superb craftsmanship. On the day the carpenters were to sail back to Japan, a large, friendly crowd gathered to bid them farewell. The guild of Swedish carpenters wanted to purchase the Japanese carpenter's tools for the Stockholm Museum, but the Japanese firmly refused payment and left the tools behind as a gift.

"You must understand that this was a real sacrifice," the Swedish professor elaborated. "For a Japanese craftsman, his tools are not mere metal and wood but have a 'spirit' that leads to creativity and perfection. His tools become an extension of his own being. The two carpenters gave their hosts their precious tools as presents, expressing indebtedness for great kindness and help."

When the carpenters landed in Japan they were astonished to see that a big crowd had assembled at the harbor to welcome them. Instead of hurrying home to their families, the two men immediately proceeded to the Double Bridge facing the Imperial Palace, where they waved the national "sun flags" and shouted three loud *Banzai!* for their Emperor.

"This search for perfection, this patriotism, this devotion to the spirit of Japan (*sushin*), to the Emperor," commented the professor, "is what constitutes the strength of the Japanese. Alas, most Westerners under-estimate their spiritual power, and I fear this ignorance will lead to a catastrophe."

The rain had stopped. Some hotel guests went for a stroll and others retired to their rooms, while a small group, including the Swedish professor and his wife, remained chatting in the dining room. The *nei-san* served hot tea and dainty triangular sandwiches. I, too, stayed behind, since I enjoyed listening to adult conversations. Eddy kept me company.

In the presence of the *nei-san* the discussion was guarded, but developed freely after they left. The talk naturally turned to present-day Japan. The professor told us that he had personally met Tatsukichi Minobe, the famous Professor Emeritus of Tokyo University accused of *lese majeste* when he termed the

Emperor an "organ" of the state.

"Minobe-San shocked the Japanese establishment," the professor said. "His book *Kempo Seigi* (Full Interpretation of the Constitution) raised subjects that were sensitive in 1935 — and are truly dangerous today. For the militarists, the Emperor is the sacred father of the nation, not part of a man-created institution and, according to them, citizens' rights are a Western concept and one they despise."

A veritable witch-hunt had been initiated against Professor Minobe, culminating in a special session of the House of Peers, where Minobe-San delivered a two-hour speech in self-defense. He stated that he had merely attempted to define — not redefine — the functions of the Emperor within the Constitution. However, the Rightists accused him of representing a dangerous, "un-Japanese" school of thought. His main enemies were the fanatic expansionists who had initiated the invasion of Manchuria.

When Professor Minobe took the platform in the House of Peers, his son, Ryokichi, was in the visitors' gallery. Many years after the war, I attended a conference in Japan in which Ryokichi participated. He had become the controversial mayor of Tokyo.

Professor Minobe's writings were banned, but clearly Japanese intellectuals valued his work because all his books sold out the day before the ban went into effect.

The Professor continued:

"I have happily lived for many years in Japan, but I never discuss my feelings with the Japanese — nor even with my most intimate friends — since this could lead to my expulsion, or worse. I do love the Japanese people and many of their unique traditions. Unfortunately, the present situation, I am convinced, is one that inevitably will lead to war with the Western powers. Now, for the first time, I am seriously considering returning with my family to Stockholm."

Surreptitiously, the Professor showed us an extract from a speech, dated July 7 (the previous month), made by Dr. H.H. Kung, China's Minister of Finance. Clearly expressing the danger facing foreign powers in China, Dr. Kung said:

The Western Powers can no longer ignore the fact that Japan's undisguised acts of lawlessness and international brigandage in the present Far-Eastern conflict constitute a real and serious menace to their own vital, political and economic interests. They must fully grasp the far-reaching international significance of these acts — namely that clearly it is Japan's firm policy to seek the conquest of China as a stepping-stone toward attempting to realize her lustful ambition of achieving mastery of Asia, hegemony in the Pacific, and eventual domination over the world.

After everyone finally dispersed, Eddy and I walked down to the beach, hoping to erase the ominous feelings the Swedish professor had evoked. Several fishermen were pulling in their catch. They had muscular legs and arms and worked very hard, but seemed cheerful in spite of their strenuous life. When I remarked on the Japanese people's diligence, dignity and uncomplaining self-sacrifice, Eddy nodded. He told me that a month ago, patriotic Japanese factory workers had willingly accepted yet another drastic wage cut so that their products could better compete on the world market.

All this gloomy conversation began to weigh upon me. The sea air was bracing and I could taste salt on my lips. Suddenly bowls of Shanghai's delicious Hazelwood ice cream flashed through my mind — my favorite "three colors" (vanilla, strawberry and chocolate) or, most delicious of all, maple nut.

"Lets run!" I urged Eddy and we dashed down the stretch of sand. We finally sat down, panting and laughing, on some rocks.

Small children, their pants rolled up, were wading in the sea. A little girl was collecting rocks, which she then dropped into a tin bucket: clang, clang, clang. Farther down, a group of young men were doing gymnastics. I decided that tomorrow I would do something new and exciting — something that was fun!

Chapter 20

The next day after tea Tamara suggested that we climb Mount Kagami (Mirror Mountain). She claimed it was an easy hike and we would be able to return to our hotel well before dark. Stupidly I agreed, forgetting her history of mischievous troublemaking. The ascent was far more difficult and time-consuming than I anticipated. Neither of us owned a watch, and when I voiced my concern, Tamara retorted with conviction:

"Don't be a sissy! The climb just seems long to you because the path is steep now. But, you'll see, it gets much flatter later on. In half an hour we'll be at the top."

When we finally stood panting on the summit, we saw stretched below us a checkerboard of rice fields, pine groves and toy-like houses. Farther beyond lay the beach, the sea, little islands, boats and ships. The setting sun bathed the landscape in delicate pearl-pink light. Soon the sun disappeared, the sky turned gray and a chilly breeze made us shiver.

"Let's go home," I said, looking around for a quick way to return.

"I know a short-cut," Tamara reassured me.

We followed a narrow path between prickly plants, but this soon ended in a clump of bushes and we had to retrace our steps. By now we had no choice but to try and find the long winding path we had taken on the way up. It grew darker and darker as we stumbled on blindly, not knowing which direction to turn. We had truly lost our way, and I began to doubt that Tamara had ever climbed Mount Kagami. Thoughts of my mother's anxiety troubled me, but Tamara gaily prattled on, giggling about her aunt, "probably chasing around like a chicken without a head," and mimicking her mother groaning about her "impossible, impossible daughter!" In fact, she appeared to be enjoying the whole thing, exclaiming:

"What fun! We can sleep overnight on the mountain. I'm sure nobody has ever done that before."

Just as I was about to retort angrily, we heard loud voices calling:

"Yoo-hoo! Ira! Tamara! Yoo-hoo!" Soon swaying lanterns appeared like glow-worms in the dark. A search party, led by my distraught mother, was looking for us.

My mother attacked me with angry words, shaming me in front of all the others, including Eddy. Silently I blinked back tears, thankful for the darkness. In the hotel, Tamara's aunt and mother greeted us with little cries of relief and concern about our cold and hunger. Tamara's aunt dragged me by the hand to their room muttering: "Poor girl, you're so upset! I know Tamara is the bad one!" The tears I had tried to hold back now started to flow.

"Have some hot tea," said Tamara's mother, bringing a large thermos bottle to the table. The aunt quickly prepared a snack of English water biscuits topped with salami. As I wiped my eyes, Tamara's mother tried to distract me with conversation.

"This sausage comes from Lohmeyer's Delicatessen in Tokyo. Don't' cry! Lohmeyer is a good German, not a Nazi. During the Great War, the Japanese [who fought against Germany] took him prisoner in China and brought him to Tokyo. He later married a Japanese woman and opened a delicatessen and restaurant. He has a very good Swiss Chef…Good. Now you're quiet. Take another biscuit. Drink some more tea. It'll warm you up."

Once during a business trip in Tokyo, Tamara's mother continued, her husband went to eat at Lohmeyer's, but had to leave when Japanese health inspectors arrived to examine the establishment. When he returned the following day, Lohmeyer (with whom he had developed a friendly relationship during his frequent visits to Japan from Shanghai) explained the reason for the rigorous search: a visit to the delicatessen the preceding afternoon by Pu-Yi, the puppet Emperor of Manchukuo. Pu-Yi had come to Japan on a state visit (actually a "command performance") and, probably feeling bored or depressed or curious, ordered his chauffeur to drive him to Lohmeyer's for a taste of the famous German *Wurst*. Mr. Lohmeyer did not recognize him but served him with his usual quiet courtesy. The following day, police, claiming to be sanitation officials, invaded the delicatessen. The purpose of their search was to determine whether an attempt had been made to poison Pu-Yi. Of course nothing was found.

The Japanese people had been kept in the dark about the new "Emperor of Manchukuo." When Pu-Yi was forcibly brought to Manchuria from Tientsin in November 1931, the Japanese press only referred to the arrival of a "distinguished visitor," a certain *Maru-Maru Sama* (Honorable Mr. X). His identity was finally revealed on March 1, 1932, when Manchukuo was proclaimed a Republic, with Pu-Yi as Regent. He was then 27 years old.

On September 15, the Japanese government gave "official recognition" to the new state it had created. On that same day, General Akira Muto, Commander of the invading Kwantung Army, signed a preliminary treaty with the former Manchuria. The new Manchukuo was declared an "independent state, organized in accordance with the free will of its inhabitants." Japanese forces, necessary "for the maintenance of national security," were to be stationed there. Manchukuo was now totally dominated by Japan. The newly appointed Chinese Cabinet Ministers were simply puppets, while true power lay in the hands of the Vice-Ministers, who were all Japanese.

On March 1, 1934, the Republic was transformed into a monarchy, headed by Pu-Yi, who was to be known henceforth as Emperor Kang-Teh.

In Shanghai, Pu-Yi was disdained by the foreigners and hated by the Chinese. Gossips whispered about his predilection for young girls and boys, his wife's opium addiction and his fawning expressions of "gratitude" towards the Japanese who held him prisoner. When Japan renamed Manchukuo's capital Changchun "Hsinking," Carroll Alcott mockingly dubbed it the seat of the "sinking" government.

Everyone laughed at the manner in which El Salvador had become the first foreign state to "officially recognize" Manchukuo. A Japanese official in Hsinking had cabled year-end holiday greetings on behalf of the "Emperor of Manchukuo" to various heads of state, all of whom ignored them — except for El Salvador, where a low-ranking government official unwittingly cabled back:

"The President of El Salvador extends felicitations to the Emperor of Manchuria."

This sufficed for the Japanese. They jubilantly publicized the first "official recognition" by a foreign government, and immediately elevated the diplomatic status of the Salvadorian Consul — a *bon vivant* who was often characterized by the Tokyo Diplomatic Corps as "the Imperial Hotel's best lobby sitter."

When Pu-Yi was invited — or rather summoned — to Tokyo, he always boarded a Japanese battleship wearing a lavish *fantasie* uniform of his own design. Thus splendidly attired, he would make self-demeaning statements upon his arrival in Japan, such as,

"I am honored to be the moon to the Mikado's sun. Together our alliance will shine over Asia."

"My husband says Manchukuo is a Japanese slave colony now," Tamara's mother told us. "More and more Japanese settlers have moved there and they're taking over everything." In 1941, the number of Japanese in Manchuria was 240,000. Now, in 1939, it had risen to 837,000.

Tamara's mother waved her finger at Tamara and added: "Don't you go repeating this now, you hear me!"

The talk about Pu-Yi had almost made me forget my earlier disgrace, but I quickly remembered upon seeing my mother's grim face when I returned to our room. To smooth matters, I swallowed my stubborn pride and promised never again to allow myself to be misled by Tamara. My sister had gone out to play with her new friend Lillian, and my mother, apparently appeased, left to chat with the Swedish professor's wife, whom she admired. Glumly I opened a book, but could not concentrate. A little while later Eddy knocked at the door and we went out on the balcony to chat.

I told him the story of Pu-Yi and Lohmeyer, whereupon he burst out:

"Pu-Yi is such a miserable coward! Surely he must know that the Japanese are using him for their own ends!"

Eddy told me that his father often traveled to Manchuria on business, to purchase animal casings and skins. According to his father, the Japanese had constructed big showy buildings in Hsinking to display their might. Hsinking was now gripped by fear. Police, troops, and armored cars were everywhere. Railway stations had become miniature fortresses, protected by pillboxes from which machine guns pointed in every direction. In trains, armed Japanese guards were on constant watch for attacks by "bandits" — the term the Japanese applied to all who opposed them.

Here, Eddy continued, the Japanese people knew nothing about the true conditions in Manchukuo. The papers published stories about the "gratitude" of the Manchurians and their warm welcome to the Japanese military. Just a year ago, in November 1938, Prime Minister Konoe had announced the establishment of a "New Order in East Asia," which would put military, political and economic activities in China and Manchukuo under Japan's "leadership." This, Konoe claimed, would save these countries from American and European exploitation.

"You will be surprised," Eddy said, "but this did not please the Japanese ultra-nationalists. They want Japan alone to rule the world, and think a 'bloc' with Manchuria and China will just be an obstacle."

Chapter 21

A letter from my father arrived after a long delay, because a strong typhoon had hit Shanghai with a wind velocity of almost 100 miles per hour. It originated in the Pacific near the islands of Yap and Guam. Fortunately, the Jesuit Fathers at the Zi-Ka-Wei Observatory in Shanghai had been aware of its impending arrival and had posted extreme storm warning signals at their semaphore tower on the Bund, thus saving many lives. At the height of the typhoon, strong winds forced tremendous surges of water from the Whangpoo River over the raised embankment, flooding the Public Gardens and even hurling tugs and sampans onto the Bund's roadway.

My father wrote that Stirling Fessenden, the American Secretary-General of the International Settlement, had resigned his post due to severe eye problems; the unfortunate man was going blind. Fessenden, whom Shanghailanders affectionately called the "Lord Mayor of Shanghai," had arrived in China in 1904, after graduating from Law School at Bowdoin College in America's northeast. He was one of very few foreigners who developed a wide circle of acquaintances among the Chinese, whose trust he had gained by respecting their beliefs and customs.

Just one year before, in 1938, he had foiled Japanese attempts to stuff ballot boxes during the annual elections for the Shanghai Municipal Council. Voting qualification for the Council was based on property ownership, and the Japanese had discovered a means to win the elections by trickery. They quickly brought in a large number of nationals from Japan, in whose name property was "bought," thus assuring their votes. Moreover, bullying Japanese campaign managers terrorized powerless Jewish refugees living in the areas under Japanese domination, forcing them to support their candidates.

Fessenden, who worriedly observed the mounting defeatism in the foreign community, took rapid action to out-maneuver the Japanese. Under his leadership, foreign companies split their properties into smaller holdings, which they then handed over to a Board of Directors in a nominal transfer. The Japanese were thus roundly defeated and were furious. How pleased they must now be at Fessenden's impending departure! The *North China Daily News* reported that, as a reward for his years of dedicated work, the Municipal Council had granted him a tax-free residence for life.

Undoubtedly, the foreigners in Shanghai were upset by Fessenden's resignation and apprehensive about the problems his successor would face with the ever-encroaching Japanese. My father, of course, did not mention this for fear of the Japanese censors. After Pearl Harbor and the Japanese occupation of the concessions, they retaliated for Fessenden's earlier actions in securing the vote. They forcefully evicted him from his house in the French Concession and he had to move to a squalid boardinghouse. By then he had become totally blind, but his loyal Chinese servants took care of him until his death.

My father also wrote that among the recently arrived refugees in Shanghai were some Russian Jews, who had been taken prisoner by Germany during the Great War and had remained in that country since that time. He said:

"Now that the German Consulate will not renew their passports, we are trying to get these people the status of stateless Russian emigrants. We hope, in this way, to be able to provide them with some kind of valid identification papers for traveling in China and neighboring countries, should the need arise."

On the whole, it was a rather short, grim letter, with much between-the-lines information. In a convoluted manner, my father hinted at new scarcities, increasing prices, and profiteering. He ended his letter by saying:

"There are many stories in the Bamboo Press which I shall tell you when y ou come home."

The Bamboo Press was what people in Shanghai called the efficient grapevine through which the Chinese obtained and passed on information, unavailable to even the best-informed and best-connected foreigners. Vanya Oakes, a local U.S. journalist, told the story of how, after Chiang Kai-shek had been kidnapped in 1936, her Boy, while serving dinner one night, suddenly announced:

"Missy, Chiang Kai-shek come back Nanking Christmas Day." — and this is indeed what happened! When Miss Oakes pressed the Boy to reveal his sources, he merely laughed:

"Any man in tea house savee." (Everyone in the teahouse knows this)...

New guests soon arrived at the Matsubara Hotel: a red-headed Scotswoman and her two jolly sons, John and Thomas, aged 13 and 11, whom my sister and I secretly nicknamed "Grasshopper" and "Rabbit." After the long journey from Tientsin, the Scotswoman suffered for several days from a migraine headache, so Mother invited the boys to join Eddy and us on a trip to a beach outside Karatsu-city. The six of us set off in a crowded old bus and finally reached our destination — a disappointingly unattractive, dirty stretch of sand.

We had barely settled down when an elderly Japanese, accompanied by a young man in student uniform, came up to us. The student, who spoke poor English, reacted to anything we said with a braying laugh, which made all of us, even my mother, giggle. Still, in spite of our repeated bursts of mirth and the linguistic obstacles, at his father's urging, the student managed to ask us the usual questions: What was our nationality? Where had we come from? What were we doing in Japan? How long would we remain? What did we think about the Japanese people?

John and Thomas mischievously volunteered the information that they lived near a lake in Scotland where a huge monster lurked, that their father was a nobleman and that they had come to Japan to look for dragons. No, they had no idea how long they would stay — perhaps forever! My mother's warning pokes did not deter them. The poor student attempted to translate their responses to his father, between brays of laughter and several puzzled "ah so desuka" (is that so?).

I would normally have felt sorry for him, but by now I had grown to resent the constant spying and prying. Just the previous evening, one of the hotel guests, a Frenchwoman from Tokyo, told us that for the past year a huge automobile had stood in front of the American Embassy there. Its tires were flat and curtains hid the interior. Everyone knew that inside the car, around the clock, Japanese policemen watched and noted down all who entered or exited the Embassy. In fact, the car remained there for almost two years and then mysteriously disappeared.

According to the Frenchwoman, most foreigners had resigned themselves to the suspicious attitude of the Japanese, and some even facilitated the work of spies so that they would bother them less! She, herself, always made a point of giving her servants a list of expected guests and of telling them exactly where she would be going, thus avoiding their irritating snooping. She did not blame her servants, poor things. It was the fault of the ubiquitous Thought Police, who forced so many nice people to act despicably. Once, when she was summoned to the police station for an investigation into an accident in which her car had allegedly been involved, she simply asked her servants to check their notes on the date in question and was easily able to prove her innocence.

Back in the hotel, a bundle of English-language newspapers

had just arrived from Tokyo, and we learned that the Vice-Minister of the Navy, Isoroku Yamamoto, who had been relieved of his post on August 2nd, had now been appointed Commander-in-Chief of the Combined Fleet.

"Do you know why he was called Isoroku?" asked Eddy. Of course, I didn't.

"Because Isoroku means 56, the age of his father when he was born," Eddy retorted triumphantly. I felt like saying: "Oh stop showing off!" but I didn't want to make him angry. Besides, I always enjoyed listening to his informative stories and I was proud to have an older boy as a friend.

According to Eddy, it was public knowledge that Army extremists had ousted Yamamoto. They had stomped around in the Navy Headquarters, complaining loudly that Yamamoto was a weakling, unable to carry out the Imperial Navy's noble tradition. Yes, it appeared that Japan too, had its own version of the Bamboo Press (which Eddy suggested should be called the "Cherry Blossom Press"). The friction between the Army and Navy, although never mentioned officially, was known to all. Rumor had it that Yamamoto's life was in danger because of his stand against Army jingoists, and that he was now being sent on sea duty to forestall assassination attempts.

We learned after the war that Yamamoto had been the originator of the Pearl Harbor attack plan. On April 18, 1943, his plane was targeted and shot down by American fighter planes.

"It is really frightening how powerful the Japanese Army has become," Eddy remarked. "They say that criticizing the Army means criticizing the Emperor; everyone, even the Navy, is afraid to challenge the Army."

Relations between the Army and the Navy had become a dangerous contest in which the Army had the upper hand. Eddy had often heard his father discussing this matter with his close friend, a very well-informed, former White Russian Colonel.

They both concluded that no foreigner could ever understand the intricacies of Japanese Army-Navy interaction.

In Shanghai too, foreign authorities had become aware of the competition between the Japanese Army and Navy. There were some 3,500 Japanese Marines in the city, and as Japanese control of Shanghai increased it became more and more evident that, behind the scenes, the Army and the Navy were skirmishing for control there too.

When we returned to the hotel, Tamara's aunt asked us all to come to their room for a treat. A new parcel of Lohmeyer's *Wurst* had arrived! Once again, Tamara's mother assured us that Lohmeyer was a "good German." Following orders by the German Embassy in Tokyo, he had displayed a swastika in his show window, but it was turned backwards to reflect his anti-Nazi sentiments.

Chapter 22

There was a full moon that etched silver streaks on the surface of the dark, softly swelling sea. My sister and I gathered on the beach together with most of the young people from the Matsubara Hotel. Our plan was to build an enormous bonfire, roast sweet potatoes and dance to records played on a hand-wound portable gramophone. Boys from the Niji Hotel, some miles up the coast, rowed down to join us, bringing along two huge watermelons as their contribution. The most popular record proved to be the "Lambeth Walk," to whose music we swirled, strode along, clapped, and shouted:

"Doin' the Lambeth Walk — Hey!"

From time to time someone would dash into the sea, then emerge, shaking off water like a puppy. Wet bodies glistened in the light of the bonfire, the burning wood gleamed red, and the smell of sweet potatoes overpowered that of brine and pines. We sadly returned to the hotel some three hours later, remembering that our precious summer vacation would soon end.

In the hotel lobby we came upon Otto and several of his friends, all dressed in khaki shorts and shirts. They were part of the *Hitler Jugend*, whom we would occasionally meet as they trudged off to some unknown destination with their fully stuffed rucksacks. They would glance arrogantly at us and we would stare back with hatred. Then, at a sign from their leader, the boys would start singing lustily in German. How I wished I had a voice and could counter with an equally passionate *La Marseillaise*!

Although many Germans in Japan, such as Mr. Lohmeyer, did not sympathize with Hitler, more and more Nazis had arrived. One who was much feared was Dr. Walter Pausch of the German Embassy. It was said that he spent most of his time compiling lists for the local police, which included alleged Japanese anti-Fascists. These persons, he proclaimed, were traitors to Japan. His collaborator was Reinhardt Schultz of the *Hitler Jugend* (most probably the "guiding light" behind Otto and his group). People whispered that 300 Nazis had been sent to Tokyo, not only to learn the Japanese language but also to try to understand the Japanese mentality, so that they could help the Embassy's Nazi staff prepare an effective propaganda campaign. All Germans visiting Japan were told that, before doing anything else, they were to bow in front of the Imperial Palace in honor of the Emperor, and immediately thereafter to extend an arm in the Nazi salute.

A new publication appeared in Tokyo, a beautifully printed and illustrated monthly, *Berlin Over Tokyo,* whose focus was Japanese art and culture. Special issues included perfectly reproduced wood-block prints. The magazine was so popular that all copies sold out almost at once. *Berlin over Tokyo* did not limit itself Japanese art and culture. Each issue also printed information on Germany, its people, its army and its industrial capacity. The articles pointed out the similarities between Germany and Japan: a love of culture, refined taste, diligence and perseverance. The implication was that Germans — unlike other Westerners — shared the qualities intrinsic to Japan.

My mother's friends in Kobe had told her, during her visit there, that German Nazis gave Japanese officials gifts of huge baskets of fruit and entertained them lavishly. At the same time, they showered them with hate propaganda against Jews, Communists, the British and the Americans. It was they who encouraged the Japanese Government to sponsor an anti-Semitic exhibit in a large department store. The Rotary Club (established in 1924) was also viciously attacked for being a "center for Jews and Communists." This created such an outcry that Prince Konoye was forced to intervene, but the pressure continued until the Rotary Club was finally disbanded. For some time daring Rotarians persisted in meeting at a newly formed "Wednesday Club," but they finally gave up.

In Shanghai, we too had been aware of the German menace. When Nazi diplomats and agents first began arriving, British-owned hotels refused to lodge them, so they set up their head-quarters in the Chinese-owned Park Hotel facing the Race Course. Eventually the Nazis managed to establish a powerful radio station, which broadcast in German, English, Italian and several Chinese dialects. They also started publishing a number of newspapers: two in Chinese, two in Japanese, one in Russian and one in English. All printed vicious articles against Jews, Americans (President Roosevelt in particular) and various British and U.S. officials on the Shanghai Municipal Council. In 1938, my father had angrily told me that, according to the Bamboo Press, the head of the Commercial Department of the Nazi Party in China had left for Berlin to collect cash to buy property in Shanghai. He intended to secure votes in the Municipal elections. Fortunately, his scheme did not succeed.

In our room I found two letters that had arrived earlier that day, one from my friend Genny Topas in Shanghai and one from Yorifumi. Genny had the prettiest handwriting of any person I knew, with the exception of my father, whose calligraphic talents I unfortunately did not inherit. She wrote that, after the typhoon, the heat and humidity returned with a vengeance and that the city was emptied of foreigners, since so many had left on vacation. She had seen several very good new movies, among them *Mr. Deeds Goes to Town,* and had read all the *Claudine* books, by our beloved French author, Colette.

Genny and I lived in Shanghai's French Concession and went to the College Municipal Français. A forerunner of the school had been established in Shanghai after the First World War. At that time, most of the students were Russian, and special French classes had been set up for them. At first, children of all ages were taught together. Gradually, however, as more French citizens settled in Shanghai and more Russian immigrants arrived, 12 classes emerged (starting with Kindergarten) and the school began to follow the curriculum prevailing in France. The language of instruction was French. In 1929, the French School officially became the College Municipal Français. French government ordinances passed in 1933 and 1934 authorized high school examinations to be held in Shanghai. Later, French *Baccalaureate* studies were instituted. Pupils took examinations identical to those in France, their papers were sent back to Paris for correction, and the diplomas awarded were fully recognized by the French Ministry of Education.

Genny and I grew up as fervent French patriots. France, we believed, was the world's foremost country in every respect: culture, justice, heroism and military superiority — there was no arguing with us!

Many of our friends went to British schools in the International Settlement and followed the British educational system. They took the Cambridge Examinations and were as convinced of Britain's superiority as we were of France's. Of course those who attended the Kaiser Wilhelm Schule were taught the superiority of Nazi ideals. Students in the American school system were less indoctrinated and appeared more jolly and carefree. Our French teachers, however, looked down on them. All the Americans cared about, they said disdainfully, was sports!

Genny complained that she hardly saw her father at all because he was perpetually attending meetings concerning the Jewish refugees. Like my father and many men in the Russian Jewish Community, Mr. Topas spent far more time at the Jewish Club than he did at home. As more and more refugees arrived and their situation became increasingly critical, many of my friends hardly ever saw their fathers, who attended endless meetings at the Club, attempting to find solutions to growing problems: Japanese pressures, a deteriorating economy, political unrest, assassinations and kidnappings.

Yorifumi's letter came in a long narrow envelope lined with pearl gray tissue paper. It was written on an almost translucent sheet of paper decorated with delicate pastel designs. Yorifumi must have worked hard on it. I guessed that he had first made a draft. How I hoped that the present military aggression and bullying would not break this gentle young man.

Yorifumi wrote:

"Foreigners cannot understand many Japanese things. For example, we worship trees, especially very old ones. People tell stories about trees that hide warriors from their enemies, in their branches and hollows."

He ended his letter:

"Please take care of yourself. The sun is too hot. You can catch sunstroke. The wind talks to me about you." He signed it: "Your Inokuchi friend, Yorifumi."

Chapter 23

It was very hot on Saturday. After lunch we joined some hotel guests who had decided to relax on canvas chaises longues
in the pine grove instead of retiring to their stuffy rooms.

John and Thomas's spinster Aunt Kate, who lived in Kobe,
arrived at the Matsubara for a week's holiday. She was a tall,
angular, plain-looking woman but her courteous manner and
melodious voice quickly made up for her ungainliness. Aunt
Kate told us that she was an English teacher who privately taught
the daughters of prominent businessmen but, alas, due to the
present "situation" (she did not elaborate), many Japanese had
stopped studying foreign languages and she had lost most of
her students. Now, for the first time in two decades, she was
seriously thinking of returning to Scotland, where she owned a
cottage in the outskirts of Edinburgh. In fact, one of the reasons why she had come to Karatsu, was to discuss the feasibil-
ity of this plan with her sister.

My eyes were half closed and I listened to the pleasant Scot-
tish lilt of Aunt Kate's voice against a background of loudly
humming cicadas. Aunt Kate's fondness and concern for her
pupils was obvious. She spoke proudly of their high moral standards and brave efforts to overcome the almost insurmount-
able obstacles of learning to speak the English language. Much
was expected of these youngsters. Not only were they trained
to be model daughters and perfect wives, but high academic
achievement was also demanded. One of her favorite pupils,
Yoshiko, had told her that when she presented herself for the
entrance examinations at a prestigious private school, there were
more than 1,000 applicants and only one in 16 could hope to
succeed. Every candidate had to undergo stringent oral testing
and then, if this first hurdle was passed, two days of difficult

written examinations would follow. Yoshiko had passed the orals but, unfortunately, failed the long written examination. She was so despondent that Aunt Kate feared that she might be contemplating suicide for having dishonored her family.

Graduation from a prominent school was of paramount importance because it influenced the direction of one's future life. Pre-examination fever seized not only students but also their parents and concerned relatives. This year, according to Aunt Kate, even highly educated parents had bought for their children a "Thomas A. Edison Headband" — a ridiculous contraption. It fit around the forehead and temple and supposedly made people "think better." The craze had first hit Tokyo and then Kobe, and purchase of them had hit a hysterical peak before the school entrance examinations began.

Although Aunt Kate had lived a long time in Japan, she was still puzzled by some aspects of the Japanese psyche.

"You never know what to expect. The Japanese mind seems to work in a different way," she said.

Once she had gone to a local carpenter to order new dining room chairs. Since the craftsman had had no experience with Western-style furniture, she gave him the exact dimensions of a comfortable chair in Tokyo's Imperial Hotel lobby.

"People must have thought I was quite mad," she said, "sitting on one chair after another to test them for comfort. They stared as I pulled a tape measure out of my bag and took precise measurements of the chair I finally selected."

After studying her sketch and specifications, the carpenter agreed to carry out the order. He calculated the cost for one chair, but increased the price per chair when he realized Aunt Kate needed six.

"But why?" cried Aunt Kate in surprise. "In my country we get a discount when we order more."

The carpenter, however, politely stood his ground. He explained that the production of six perfectly identical chairs would involve far more exacting work than making only one.

"Perhaps he was right," sighed Aunt Kate, "but they do seem to follow a logic different from ours. No wonder that when they speak of themselves, the Japanese say *ware-ware Nihon-jin* (we, the Japanese), to differentiate them from the non-Japanese, or foreigners. They truly believe the saying:

"There are three ways to do things: the right way, the wrong way, and the Japanese way."

At this point a Danish lady, whose husband owned an export business in Yokohama, interjected rather heatedly that a foreigner in Japan, no matter how much he loved the country and how well he learned the Japanese language and customs, would always remain a *gaikokujin* (foreign-country person), an outsider. Indeed, most Koreans born in Japan, who could hardly be distinguished from the Japanese themselves, were never fully accepted in society. Descendants of Korean craftsmen brought to Japan more than three centuries ago were still regarded as aliens. It was almost impossible for a foreigner to acquire Japanese nationality and even if he achieved this, he was never granted the status and full rights of a "true" Japanese. One of the Danish lady's friends, a Frenchwoman married to a Japanese artist in Tokyo, had finally become a Japanese citizen. Nevertheless, the Military Police would frequently "drop in" at the artist's home and question him repeatedly about his *gaikokujin* wife. The fact that she was now legally Japanese obviously meant nothing.

"The Japanese simply don't trust outsiders," the Danish lady contended.

Her husband had told her that even naturalized citizens, like foreign nationals, were automatically barred from engaging in any business or industry connected, directly or indirectly, with Japan's defense. Further, all foreigners in Japan had to be fingerprinted (a law that remained in force until the end of 1992).

The Danish lady's story was followed by a short silence, as the *nei-san* arrived with refreshments. Plans were then discussed for a sukiyaki party, a farewell gathering before the holiday season ended.

My mother became very fond of Aunt Kate and went with her on long hikes, since Aunt Kate's sister, who was somewhat older and far less energetic, preferred sitting on the beach. According to my mother, the Scotswoman was *"zamechatelnaya"* (splendid) — kind, educated and open minded. Kate seemed to enjoy my mother's quick wit, sharp insight and positive attitude toward life.

My mother was indeed a good storyteller, and Aunt Kate listened with rapt attention to her, forgetting for the moment her personal dilemma and the darkening political atmosphere. I watched with delight as she flung back her head and burst into open-mouthed child-like laughter at my mother's humorous account of the "English saddle."

This incident, typical of the irresponsible lifestyle led by the privileged foreigners in Shanghai in the 1930's, had made the rounds of all the swanky clubs. At the time, most Westerners made purchases by simply signing a "chit," an I.O.U. scribbled on a slip of paper that would be paid at the end of the month. In this instance an Englishman had bought an expensive, imported saddle at a high-class British department store, and had forgotten to sign his "chit." Noting that the saddle had been delivered to the Race Club, the store manager checked the names of club members who had accounts with the store. He identified 21 possible buyers. The manager then instructed his accounting department to send each one of them a bill, assuming that the gentleman owing the money would pay the bill, while the others would claim a mistake had been made. Imagine his surprise when only nine customers telephoned to deny that they had bought a saddle; twelve had nonchalantly paid the invoice!

Aunt Kate's hobby was to collect *ukiyoe*, Japanese wood-block prints. She showed us one she had brought her sister as a gift. It was portrait of a *kabuki* actor and was printed on paper made by hand from the inner bark of a mulberry tree. She told us that this life-long passion was sparked when, in 1925, she visited the first wood-block print exhibit ever held in Japan.

"The Japanese used to consider *ukiyoe* a low form of art," Aunt Kate said, "but foreigners loved it."

In the 1880's, Henri Vever, the famous Parisian jeweler and painter, started collecting Japanese wood-block prints and eventually bought more than 8,000, by artists such as Hokusai, Tokoyuni and Hiroshige. Soon *ukiyoe* aficionados began to meet monthly in a Paris restaurant for *diners japonisants* to discuss their latest acquisitions. By the end of the 19th century, interest in *ukiyoe* had reached a peak in France and spread to other European countries. By the time the Japanese finally realized the artistic value of wood-block prints, it was too late; the best were in foreign hands. Fortunately for them, however, Henri Vever was a man who believed that the true place of art was its country of origin. In the early 1920's, he agreed to sell 3,000 top-quality prints to a Tokyo businessman. This gentleman, in turn, generously donated the *ukiyoe* to a bank and they arranged the public exhibition, the one that Aunt Kate had been lucky enough to visit. Later, in a burst of patriotic self-sacrifice, the bank presented its entire *ukiyoe* collection to the Imperial Household.

In spite of cultural differences and the growing pressure from the Thought Police, there was no doubt that Aunt Kate loved Japan and dreaded her impending departure. She told us of the many kindnesses she had experienced throughout her sojourn in Kobe, of the high regard in which teachers were held by students, parents and Japanese society and of the Japanese people's sensitivity and patience.

Aunt Kate said: "The Japanese are so considerate! When I was ill last year, all my pupils, without exception, came to visit me, bringing flowers and beautifully wrapped little gifts. My young maid, Yoko-San, treated me like a most devoted daughter. She would send her brother across the city on his bicycle to buy the special "spring chicken for foreigners" and cook me a heavenly consommé. You know, most chicken in Japan tastes fishy because the poultry is fed fishmeal; only a small number of farmers around Kobe fed expensive grain to their chickens in order to make the meat palatable to finicky Europeans. Yoko-San, worried about my loss of appetite, would spoon-feed me this special chicken broth, a light gold liquid without a single droplet of fat."

Aunt Kate sighed and continued:"Such polite people, the Japanese! They never laugh at my clumsiness, the way I mangle Japanese words, my idiosyncrasies. I shall miss them so."

Chapter 24

My father did not openly express concern in the letters he wrote us, but deep worry filtered in between the lines. Often in Shanghai he had commented that the world was being drawn into a maelstrom of military ambition in the Far East, a danger to which the Great Powers appeared indifferent. Many people in Shanghai — both Chinese and Westerners — shared his apprehensions, but somehow failed to impress them upon the powers-that-be in London, Paris and Washington. Vanya Oakes, an American journalist stationed in Shanghai, wrote later of her despair:

... I devoted my time in the Orient to one frantic and consistent plea: Wake up America! There was no longer any doubt in my mind that the Western Powers were going to be struck, and struck hard. To say that my pleas fell on disinterested ears is putting it exceedingly mildly. I received from the homeside offices of the newspapers and magazines for which I was writing, calm advice to pull myself together, that I was becoming hysterical, and that if I could not acquire more of the characteristic tranquility of the Far East, I had better leave for home...

For the time being, however, Japan's "invincible" army seemed to be experiencing difficulties — not that this fact was ever reflected in the Japanese news media. Our information came from a White Russian gentleman from Tientsin, Peotr Petrovich Russanov, who had arrived in Karatsu to spend ten days with his vacationing family. He dealt in furs and traveled quite extensively in Manchukuo and China. He had learned from his Chinese business associates that Japan's Kwantung Army was not faring well. We had also noted the increasing numbers of boxes with the ashes of dead soldiers were being regularly delivered to relatives at Japanese train stations.

Mr. Russanov hated and mistrusted the *prokliatiye* (cursed) Soviets. His suspicions were soon justified. In the summer of 1939, news of a Russo-German Non-Aggression Pact hit the world like an explosion. On August 23, Molotov and Ribbentrop had met in Moscow and 24 hours later an agreement was signed between the U.S.S.R and the German Reich. Each country had committed not to attack the other, not to support a third power that acted belligerently toward the other and not to join any alliance aimed directly or indirectly at the other. Five days later, a shocked Japanese Cabinet resigned. The Japanese angrily accused Germany of breaking the Anti-Comintern Pact, which Japan had signed with the very same Foreign Minister Ribbentrop in November 1936, against the Soviet Union and its system of international communism. Unfortunately, this did not lead to better relations between Japan and United States or Great Britain.

Peotr Petrovich told us his story. He had arrived as a disillusioned young man in Harbin after the collapse of the anti-communist movement in Siberia. His father, a wealthy landowner, had been murdered and he, his mother and sister — together with thousands of fleeing refugees — had crossed the Manchurian border into Harbin, a city under Chinese administration. Here, the Russian expatriates worked very hard to create an environment similar to one that had existed in Russia during less turbulent times. Onion-domed churches were built, newspapers published, schools and colleges founded, theater, opera and operetta companies established, and a circus performed every night to a crowd of enthusiastic spectators. He dramatically recited for us the words of the popular Harbin poet, Aleksey Achair:

"Because our Motherland drove us away,
We carry her light with us..."

Piotr Petrovich sighed and continued: "All this wonderful cultural life, the balls, swimming in the Sungari River, the picnics, the Orthodox Christmas and Easter celebrations, it all ended in 1932.

"What a year! In August the water of the Sungari rose so high that we had to use rowboats to make our way around the city. More than 100,000 people were left homeless, without food and drinking water. And then the worst happened. The Japanese invaded Northern Manchuria and occupied Harbin by force.

"Oh, they had many excuses: they were saving the Chinese from the Communists, defending the independence of Manchukuo against Western exploitation, and liberating Asia for the Asians. Most Japanese soldiers in Harbin were thugs. The city deteriorated, drugs and gambling houses appeared everywhere, and kidnappings for ransom became common. Of course, the foreigners who could do so all left. I managed, with great difficulty, to bring my family to Tientsin. Da! takovaya jizn! [Yes! such is life!] We White Russians seem doomed to flee from one country to another. It never ends. Never..."

Developments were ominous, yet our comfortable, pleasant life continued at the Matsubara Hotel. The *nei-san* spoiled the guests, smiled and bowed; youngsters chattered at meals, and plans were made for bonfires, sukiyaki parties, hikes and day-trips. After all, we were all on summer vacation — perhaps the last one before a worldwide cataclysm.

Chapter 25

There was a whiff of autumn in the air. In the early mornings and evenings the steady breeze from the sea had a cold bite. Jellyfish invaded, and the sea swept them onto the beach, where they rotted in untidy piles, mixed with long, viscous, smelly strips of seaweed and dead starfish. After breakfast I was up in our room writing a letter to Genny Topas when a pine cone sailed in through the open window. It was Eddy trying to catch my attention.

"Come on down!" he shouted. "We're renting a boat to row out to the Seven Caves".

I pushed my letter paper back into the drawer and ran outside. Our vacation was coming to an end. The atmosphere at the hotel had changed from that of a jolly holiday to one of heavy-hearted preparation for departure. How sad to think that I might never see Eddy again, that our enchanted summer was almost over and that the world might be on the brink of war — belying the "historic fact" taught at the College Municipal: "La Grande Guerre est la dernière guerre" (The Great War is the last war). Suddenly, every moment became precious, was to be savored, remembered and stored away. No, I would not read, not write letters, not lie in my room. I would spend all my remaining free hours in Karatsu, wading in the sea, roaming in the villages, climbing hills, assimilating the colors, smells, flowing movement of this lovely resort.

My mother, sister, her friend Lillian, Lillian's aunt, Tamara, Eddy and I piled into a large, flat-bottomed boat. The two lean Japanese boatmen rowed rhythmically. When we distanced ourselves from the shore, the sea became choppy and Lilian's aunt got very seasick. I felt queasy but pride made me hide my discomfort. The rest were chattering loudly and to my surprise my mother, who had been so ill on our voyage to Nagasaki, appeared not to suffer the effects of the rocking boat. I noticed how much good this vacation had done her: She was tanned, her eyes shone, her whole being sparkled. I had never thought about her age, but now I noticed she looked like a young, care-free girl.

The boatmen rowed us into a cave so deep that nobody knew where it ended — at least so said a pamphlet someone had brought along. There was a stillness, a feeling of isolation from the rest of the world. All one could hear was the gentle lapping of wavelets against the rocks. In the semi-darkness, Eddy's arm briefly encircled my back — the first time he had demonstrated any affection for me.

"No matter what happens," I told myself, "I'll treasure this day, I'll remember it for ever and ever."

When we returned to the beach, Eddy and I walked along silently, side by side, and came across a group of young Japanese soldiers roasting potatoes over a bonfire. They soon surrounded us and one bespectacled youngster, probably not trusting himself to speak English, scribbled with his finger on the sand:

"English? American? German?"

Eddy countered writing in capital letters:

"NO. WHITE RUSSIAN. JEWISH."

The soldier looked puzzled. One of his comrades pulled a box camera out of his knapsack and took our picture. Waving good-bye, we waded along the shore and met Petr Petrovich taking a walk on the sand.

"Ach, rebiata kak chudno zdes!" (Ah, kids how wonderful it is here!), he cried enthusiastically as he joined us. He had watched us chatting with the soldiers, he said, and hoped we had been circumspect. Eddy quickly reassured him that we had. The conversation turned to the Japanese people's belief in

Emperor Hirohito's divine mission, his sacred destiny, and *Yamato Daiichi* (the spirit of Japan). Both Eddy and Mr. Russanov seemed well informed. I, knowing nothing, listened in silence.

Piotr Petrovich told us about the sadistic treatment Japanese recruits suffered in boot camp. Petty officers regularly beat them all over their bodies with such violence that men frequently fainted. Nobody protested. All soldiers stoically accepted the "discipline" that would mold them into fierce warriors for the Emperor.

Piotr Petrovich told us that in 1923 there had been an attempt to assassinate Hirohito when he was Prince Regent. The attacker was a young anarchist named Daisuke Namba, who fired twice at the royal carriage but missed his target. All Japan was outraged. Daisuke Namba was hanged one year later. He claimed he had had no accomplices. It was not difficult to convince the public that he had acted alone. Supporting him would have meant political suicide for Japan's left. Nevertheless, reports persisted that he had shouted *"Banzai* to the workers!" just before his execution. (Some 45 years later, the name Daisuke Namba was assumed by the communist, Kozo Okamoto, when he carried out his bloody terrorist attack at the Tel Aviv airport.)

In our hotel room, my mother was reading a letter from my father — the last one he wrote, since we would soon be returning home. His entire thoughts now concentrated on the Jewish refugees. Many were confused and feared to stray from their lodgings because they could speak neither Chinese nor English, which was Shanghai's *lingua franca*. He hoped this situation would improve – and it eventually did. As time passed, many refugees recovered their self-confidence and ventured into the shops, the markets, and the parks.

It must indeed have been a traumatic experience, my father

wrote, to flee from Europe to distant China and live in slum-
like, makeshift housing. Some 1500 refugees, mostly those
without families, were concentrated in *Heime* (group homes).
This made the distribution of food, clothing and other necessi-
ties simpler and cheaper, but provided a depressing atmosphere.
Local Jewish families offered to take 150 refugee children into
their homes, but only 25 refugee families agreed to separation
from their children. No matter how miserable their housing and
circumstances, they chose to keep their children with them and
their family intact. My father could identify with their feelings.

The International Red Cross in Shanghai had promised to
donate money to the local Jewish relief committees, but their
contributions were insignificant because most of the Red Cross
funds had been earmarked for destitute Chinese. Still, the Red
Cross had been able to provide several jobs for refugee doctors
in the interior of China, where medical care was desperately
needed.

Sir Victor Sassoon, a local Sephardi tycoon, had generously
established a Rehabilitation Fund of $150,000 to finance small
business ventures for Jewish refugees. Thanks to this donation,
a refugee doctor my father knew had been able to open a
practice. An acquaintance of my uncle started a small bistro.
The American Joint Distribution Committee, that later was to
play a historic role in saving Shanghai's Jewish refugees, was
unable as yet to commit itself to support the refugees financially.
(This came about later, after we had left Japan, in September
1939.)

"The Nazis have created a human catastrophe," wrote my
father. "What is the world waiting for? Why doesn't anyone
help? How much can we, a small group of Jews, possibly do?"

Jews throughout the world reacted with horror to the news
that 900 German Jewish refugees, who had left Europe on the
S.S. St. *Louis,* had been refused entry by several countries, in-

cluding the United States. They were forced to return to Europe. My father sent us a clipping of an English translation of an article in the German newspaper, *Weltkampf.* A Nazi journalist wrote:

"We are saying openly that we do not want the Jews, while the democracies keep on claiming that they are willing to receive them — then leaving their guests out in the cold. Aren't we 'savages' better men after all?"

My father ended his letter on a more pleasant note. He told us that a Polish refugee from Byalostok, one Yehoshu Rappoport, had become a great cultural asset to the Russian Jewish Community in Shanghai.

"He is a brilliant writer and excellent lecturer both in Russian and in Yiddish," wrote my father. "Whenever he is scheduled to speak, people flock to hear him. I am so happy that, in spite of the menace surrounding us, people still remain interested in intellectual matters and are eager to learn, to discuss, to try to understand one another."

(In an unusual twist of fate, a young American came to China on a diplomatic assignment shortly before this book was published and, after reading the draft, informed the editor that the learned gentleman was his grandfather!)

Chapter 26

Kolia, one of the Nikko Hotel boys who lived in Kobe, came over in the evening with a pile of newspaper clippings. His hobby was collecting "funny" items published in the local papers, humorous either because of their content or their language. Eddy and I sat with him at the far end of the dining room and roared with laughter.

"Please let me copy some of these articles," I begged. "My friends in Shanghai will love them!" After some hesitation, Kolia agreed and let me keep his treasured clippings for several days.

My favorite story told how the renowned Japanese publisher of the *Yomiuri* newspapers, Matsutaro Shoriki, had sent publisher William Randolph Hearst an ancient Samurai armor as a gift. Mr. Hearst, advised by his famous explorer friend Harold Jefferson Coolidge, reciprocated by shipping three bison to the Tokyo Zoo. Two were females and one male. A local English-language newspaper explained:

"Bison very fleet animals. Even the fleetest horses cannot overtake them...Also it is said they are more rough than lions and tigers."

When the animals arrived, the Mayor of Tokyo declared an official "Buffalo Week," during which the price of bus tickets to the zoo was cut in half. Thousands rushed to see the exotic animals. A delegation of schoolchildren presented a bouquet to the male whereupon, according to a newspaperman, "the distinguished arrival accepted the tribute by eating the flowers."

Alas, in spite of all the love showered upon the bison and the best of care, provided by the imperial household veterinarians, one died unexpectedly. The tragic event was reported in the

Japanese press as follows:

One of the bison which the Newspaper King of America, Mr. William Randolph Hearst, sent to Japan and which came to Japan on good-will mission, died without seeing beautiful cherry blossom, despite our every effort to restore its health... Said bison was attended by Zoo doctors and she understood as being a slight cold. At 8:45 A.M. she died, despite our every care and treatment. She died of acute bronchitis, bronchopneumonia and septicemia. Animals suffering from such is hard to taken care of and in most cases dead.

Passing through seasonal molting period, she can hardly be stuffed, but in view she is such rare animal to be possessed here, her skeleton will be preserved in Tokio Imperial University...

Upon hearing the outpourings of grief in Japan when the bison died, Hearst sent a replacement, whose arrival was welcomed in the Tokyo press.

The new Miss Bison...entered into her bridegroom's house where the Bison family has been longing for her joining.

On her arrival at the Zoo on a large truck, a large number of girls and boys who were visitors at the Zoo, welcomed the bride. Under the instruction of Mr. Koga, chief of the Zoo, men opened a large cage door and Miss Bison, 120-*kan* [990 lbs.] in weight, with her brown costume, slowly walked into her new home.

She is as large as male Bison, her groom, and she is larger than her sister-in-law Bison...

The following morning was windy and gray — definitely not a day for the beach — so I asked Eddy if he would accompany me to the city to buy a scrapbook for the clippings and copies of articles I had collected during the summer.

The rickety bus was more overcrowded than usual, for a reason we understood when we got out at Karatsu station. A "Military Exhibit" was being held in a neighboring two-story building. Banners with ideograms and flags promoted the important event. A long line of people waited patiently to enter, most carrying folded wax paper umbrellas in the expectation of rain.

"Let's have a look!" Eddy said, and we got in line.

An elderly Japanese woman in front of us smiled in a kindly way and gestured us to go ahead, saying:

"Dozo! Dozo!" (Please, please!)

We refused, with many *domo arigato* (thank you very much).

When we finally entered, we saw graphs, maps, charts and military equipment, including two small tanks, machine-guns mounted on khaki colored motorcycles, bombs and torpedoes. In a special room there were miniature life-like displays of Japanese soldiers battling in jungles, mountains, rivers, deserts, and snow. How "clean" and heroic war was made to appear, how far from the filth, pain and misery I had observed in China. The final glass case, however, did bring spectators closer to reality. In it was the bloodstained uniform of a soldier killed in action. On a little easel above the case stood a snapshot of the young man who had allegedly worn the uniform when he died. He could have been Yorifumi's brother, with his clear unsmiling look, finely curved brows and sensitive mouth. On a small adjacent table stood two white ceramic bowls. One contained sweet smelling incense from which bluish vapors emanated and the other coins that visitors had contributed towards the war effort.

The centerpiece of the exhibit was a miniature model of a Japanese city, a display that Eddy whispered that he had already seen in Tokyo. It lay on a large table around which visitors were crowded three deep. There were tiny houses, streets, parks and sparkling lights. Suddenly a siren wailed and the miniature city was plunged into darkness. Tiny "enemy" planes appeared, moving along a thin overhead wire. They were quickly pinpointed in the beams of tiny searchlights. Then we heard the rat-a-tat-tat of anti-aircraft guns, Japanese planes zoomed down, and the invaders fled. The city burst into light once again, martial music sounded, and everyone clapped.

When we went out, Eddy wondered why so many different terrains and weather conditions had been exhibited. Were the Japanese preparing for war in different parts of the world? Then interrupting himself, he said:

"Let's forget about all this." Shamelessly he took my hand and we rambled around, smiling at each other, ate watery ice cream, watched acrobats tumbling on the pavement, and singing soldiers marching to an unknown destination. At a stationery store, we found a scrapbook I liked. The cover was of a light colored wood and the pages pale beige. Before returning to our hotel, we rested on a bench in a small park and ate the *bento* lunch the *nei-san* had thoughtfully prepared for us. I wished the day would never end.

Chapter 27

Huge dark waves were thrashing and bursting against the shore. Tamara and I, wearing cardigans over our swimsuits, sat staring at the threatening green-black sea. She was leaving that evening for China. For once she was silent, thoughtful, buried within herself. Eddy had left the day before. How quiet everything was without him. He really was the bond between us all. I already missed the little frown between his eyebrows when he concentrated, his fleeting shy smile, the sight of his tanned muscular body and the wisp of hair he kept pushing back from his forehead. I remembered the feel of his hand discreetly patting my cheek and the grasp of his strong fingers as he helped me up steep rocks.

In an effort to soothe our troubled spirits — evidenced by the unusual hush that had descended on the remaining guests — the hotel cook had prepared a delectable sukiyaki lunch. All the youngsters, with the exception of the two German boys, gathered on a *tatami* mat. As dessert was served, our popular manager presented a little gift to each of us. The boys received miniature Samurai paper-cutter swords, packed in slim bamboo boxes, and the girls tiny brocade-covered address books, wrapped in speckled tissue paper topped with a tiny pink silk rose.

After lunch, our entire group set out for a stroll in the village, where we came upon an excited crowd outside a hardware store. A man had tried to steal some merchandise and the storekeeper had managed to grab him. During the tumult, a uniformed policeman arrived and handed his name-card to the shopkeeper. At that time, policemen did not wear badges or numbers, but instead introduced themselves as businessmen would. The officer's face was menacing, his voice intimidating. His short, sharp words lashed at the quaking thief. We quickly walked away from the painful scene.

No wonder the poor fellow was terrified. He knew that he would be jailed for as long as the police decided, perhaps one or two years, before his case was finally heard in court. We had all heard of the dreadful conditions in Japanese jails. Prisoners were forced to kneel in their cells, their arms had to remain folded, and only one position was permitted: back to the door, face to the wall. Talking, smoking, reading, and writing were strictly forbidden. No lawyers were assigned to those jailed. The police would eventually demand a signed confession of guilt — an order to which prisoners would, unsurprisingly, comply. Frequently, the innocent admitted to imaginary crimes with feigned repentance.

Eddy had told me about the case of a Tokyo deliveryman accused of stealing sewing machine parts. The factory manager who had placed the order claimed he had never received the merchandise. As a result, the deliveryman was fingerprinted, thrown into jail and there, admitted to having sold the undelivered merchandise. His confession included a detailed account of how he had spent the stolen money drinking and gambling. Six months later, the sewing machine parts were found during a routine factory inventory. Someone had neglected to inform the manager of their arrival. The innocent deliveryman, who had needlessly suffered for so long, was set free. Eddy assumed that neither apology nor compensation were ever made to the innocent man.

Since it was Tamara's last day, we all agreed to do whatever she wished. She decided upon a short bus ride to a village known for the delicious yellow watermelon. As usual, the bus was crowded, and we noticed that Japanese women gave up their seats to men in uniform; in 1939 soldiers were the objects of tender respect in Karatsu. The passengers nodded at us in a friendly manner as we all swayed together while the driver careened down the dusty road. My feelings were confused. I loved the Japanese people, and yet I hated their excesses in China, their cruel military actions, and their repressive government.

Later that evening, as we said good-bye to Tamara, I realized that, in spite of her mischief making, I had grown very fond of her. Our misadventure on Mount Mirror now belonged to the distant past, our summer vacation was now ending and we would soon be returning to overcrowded, war-jittery Shanghai to face an uncertain future.

News filtering in from China continued to be depressing. The Great Powers (the United States, Great Britain, and France) seemed to be acceding to the never-ending Japanese encroachment. Japanese soldiers were maltreating and intimidating the Chinese at whim, foreign newspapermen were being harassed and radio broadcasts jammed. The situation was rapidly deteriorating.

Chapter 28

On August 23, after Molotov and Ribbentrop had signed the new Non-Aggression Pact, Stalin drank a toast to Hitler at the ensuing banquet — which celebrated the virtual division of all of Eastern Europe into German and Russian spheres. Everyone now expected Poland to be attacked and all of the hotel guests were worried and subdued. Should the feared event occur, Britain and France would have no choice but to come to Poland's defense.

Enjoying our Karatsu vacation, we of course knew nothing of a Japanese Consul, assigned to Kovno (Lithuania) since March of that year, who would soon become instrumental in saving several thousand Polish Jews. Among them was a slender, inconspicuous man named Josef Shimkin, who was later to become my parents' friend.

Senpo Sugihara, a second grade interpreter (some say intelligence agent), was selected to serve as Consul in Kovno, partly because of his fluency in Russian. At first, Consul Sugihara, his wife and sons led a pleasant, uneventful life in their little villa, but they were soon shocked into awareness of the Nazi's anti-Semitic terror that had blanketed Europe. Hundreds of desperate Polish Jews gathered in front of their home, clamoring for visas to Japan. No other consulates in Europe were prepared to issue visas to Jews. Japan was their last and only hope.

Horrified by the enormity of the tragedy unfolding around him, Sugihara began exploring possible means to save the Jews. His repeated requests to Tokyo for permission to issue visitors' visas to Jewish refugees were denied, but Sugihara was authorized to stamp transit visas, valid for travel via Japan. However, this would only be possible if the Jews held entry permits to another, final destination. Unfortunately, in 1939 entry permits from most countries were almost impossible for Jews to obtain.

Sugihara found a collaborator to resolve the dilemma. Contrary to regulations in force at the time, the new Dutch Consul in Kovno, Jan Zwartendjik, unlike his pro-Nazi predecessor, agreed to stamp the Polish Jews' documents with permits to enter Curacao, in the Netherlands' Antilles. He did so although he knew full well that, officially, a Landing Permit from the Governor of the island had to be first obtained, a request the Governor would most certainly deny.

Determined not to lose any more time, Sugihara simply began to issue transit visas on his own authority. At first he stamped passports, but later he issued transit visas on whatever papers the refugees handed him, even mere sheets of paper that bore the words "Curacao - No Visa Required." (Due to the great upheaval in Europe, many Jews carried no official documents whatsoever.) The role of these fearless and noble men, Kenpo Sugihara and Jan Zwartendjik, in the rescue of European Jews has only recently been fully recognized.

Josef Shimkin later told my parents that he had been involved in a clandestine operation to save Jews by smuggling them out of the Nazi-occupied areas. In the process he had become an expert at forging documents. Speed was imperative. No matter how fast Sugihara was able to issue his Japanese transit visas, the time was running out for thousands of Jews. Shimkin, with Sugihara's knowledge, began feverishly to falsify Japanese transit permits. Eventually, thousands of forged visas turned up. Sometimes Jews landed in Japan with identical papers, obvious copies of each other. Opinions vary as to why the Japanese authorities accepted them for entry.

The refugees hoped that if they managed to reach Vladivostok and board ships to Japan, local Jews would somehow be able to help them. This assumption proved to be correct. Kobe's small community of Jews did indeed respond heroically. At risk to themselves they intervened with the Japanese authorities and convinced them to allow the refugees to land. They prepared 20 houses for emergency lodging, organized kosher kitchens and the distribution of clothing. Eventually, these Jewish refugees left Kobe for Shanghai, where no entry papers were required. That is where Shimkin met my parents.

Josef Shimkin retained good memories of Japan. Many years later he returned, opened a business in Tokyo and married a Japanese woman. He died there in 1993 and is buried in the cemetery in Yokohama.

While this amazing story was unfolding in distant Europe, we in Karatsu were making our final preparations for the end of our happy summer vacation. The weather had turned chilly and on the beach the wind blew the sand into little clouds. All the jellyfish had disappeared so now we could plunge into the cold waves without fear of being stung. The nip of autumn was in the air as taxis arrived to drive hotel guests and their luggage to train stations. Our handsome Japanese hotel manager bowed his farewells and the gentle maids, now no longer wearing their light cotton kimono, wiped away sentimental tears. As for us, we waved good-bye with a sinking feeling that we would never return — at least not as carefree vacationing youngsters.

Chapter 29

At the end of August, my mother, sister and I also took a taxi and headed for the train station on the first lap of our return journey to Shanghai. We looked for the last time at the peaceful Japanese panorama through the rather grimy windows of our compartment, bought the *bento* lunches now so familiar to us, drank green tea from little pottery pots, and thanked the vendors with an unselfconscious *domo arigato*. The ride to Nagasaki was a long *sayonara* to a country we had come to love — in spite of the spying, the prying and the Japanese values that were sometimes so strange and utterly different from ours. While my mother stayed behind in Nagasaki to complete formalities, my sister and I boarded a launch to the *S.S. Chenonceaux*, a French liner belonging to the Messageries Maritimes Line. On this trip, we had a clean, airy cabin with three bunks and a porthole through which we could glimpse the flat, almost motionless sea. As he carried our suitcases, a young French steward proudly declared that the *Boche* (insulting word for German) would never dare to set foot on French soil.

"On va les avoir!" (We'll get them!), he crowed.

"Bien sûr!" (Of course!), I replied with absolute certainty. My teachers at the College Municipal in Shanghai had thoroughly convinced me that France's army was invincible.

We washed and changed in our tiny bathroom and, hearing a gong, went up for tea. A black grand piano graced the dining room with its polished splendor. An elegant chandelier cast its benign light on us. The tables were covered with spotless white damask. Flirtatious young Frenchmen served us tiny, delicious, triangular sandwiches, biscuits, *gateaux*, coffee and hot chocolate.

After tea, my sister and I rushed to examine the S.S.

Chenonceaux. There was a shop, a library, ping-pong tables, chess and card games. On the decks, passengers relaxed in comfortable chairs, cozily wrapped in colorful plaid blankets. A young sailor stopped to talk with us. He told us that he was 18 years old and that his name was Papillon (butterfly in French). He was free that evening and, if we wished, we could meet him in a corner of the deck and he would play his guitar and sing for us. We promised to ask our mother.

During dinner, bottles of red wine, which we did not drink, stood on the tables, along with baskets filled with crunchy warm rolls, which we devoured. The sea was calm and no one on board appeared to be seasick. The food disappeared quickly and second helpings were served. To our relief, mother agreed that my sister and I could meet Papillon. We ran up to the deck. A cool breeze was blowing and the sky was studded with stars. Our ship was a comforting, all-encompassing cocoon and I felt coddled, safe, protected.

Papillon stood at the appointed place with his guitar. He smiled with delight as we came up. Accompanying himself on his guitar, he sang:

> Il pleut sur la route
> Dans la nuit j'écoute
> Au bruit de chaque pas
> Le son de ta voix.

> It's raining on the road
> In the night I am listening
> At the noise of each step
> For the sound of your voice.

There was sadness and longing in Papillon's pleasant voice. For a girl friend? For his family? For France? Japan seemed far,

far away.

That night when my sister and I went to bed our excitement prevented us from falling asleep. We lay listening to the music that drifted down to our cabin from the dance band in First Class. We could hardly wait for morning to come so that we could roam around the ship, play ping-pong and look through the French books in the ship's library.

After breakfast, we rushed off — but stopped short at the entrance to the main lounge. A silent crowd was reading an outsized notice on a blackboard placed high on an easel. Large handwritten letters chalked on it announced:

WAR IN EUROPE!

Our glorious summer vacation was at an end. It was the last for many years to come.